COTTRELL

*Cottrell Park, St. Nicholas,
Vale of Glamorgan*

COTTRELL

*Cottrell Park, St. Nicholas,
Vale of Glamorgan*

John Richards

Published by: Cottrell Park, St. Nicholas,
Cardiff, CF5 6TR.
ISBN: 0 9535582 0 7

© John Richards, 1999

The right of John Richards to be identified as the author of this work has been asserted by him in accordance with the Copyright, Designs and Patents Act 1988.

Designed and produced by:
A.R.B. Advertising and Graphic Design,
Cardiff.
Type: Palatino 10/13pt.
Printed by: South Western Printers, Caerphilly.

All rights reserved. No part of this publication may be reproduced, stored in a retrieval system, or transmitted, in any form or by any means, without the prior permission of both the publisher and the copyright holder.

COTTRELL

Foreword

I am delighted to be able to introduce this, the first history of the Cottrell estate.

People connected with Cottrell Park have travelled, over a period of 500 years, to many parts of the world: the Caribbean, colonial America, Hudson's Bay, India, Africa and the Mediterranean.

In these pages you will find piracy, exploration, battles, revolution and civil war, as well as more everyday human tragedies and triumphs.

I am sure that both visitors to the Golf Club and members of our local community will enjoy reading this fascinating book.

David Johns-Powell
Managing Director

Acknowledgements

The author wishes to thank the following for providing information and/or illustrations:

Bodleian Library, Oxford; Bridgeman Art Library; Bristol City Archives; British Library; British Red Cross Archive; Buckinghamshire Record Office; Cambridge University Collection of Air Photographs; Cambridge University Library; Cardiff City Library; Cheshire Record Office; City of Cork Library; Dr. J. David Hughes (Bedford); Beryl Dolan (London); Derbyshire Record Office; East Sussex Record Office; Brigadier A.I.H. Fyfe, D.L. (Somerset Light Infantry); Georgia Department of Archives and History (Atlanta); Georgia Historical Society (Atlanta); Georgia Humanities Council (Atlanta); Glamorgan-Gwent Archaeological Trust; Glamorgan Record Office; Gloucestershire Library and Record Office; The Librarian, Hatfield House; Herefordshire Record Office; Household Cavalry Museum; Hudson's Bay Company Archives (Winnipeg); Imperial War Museum; Inverness Museum; Harvey H. Jackson (Jacksonville State University, Alabama); Margaret John (St. Fagans); Leicestershire Record Office; Llantwit Major Parish Council; Thomas Lloyd; Mr. and Mrs. Murray McLaggan; Pauline McGillivray (Clan Chattan Association); Military Museum of Devon and Dorset (Dorchester); Monmouth Museum; Andrew Morgan (Past President, Welsh Golfing Union); Museum of London; Museum of Welsh Life (in particular: the Archivist and the Librarian); National Archives of Canada; National Horseracing Museum (Newmarket); National Library of Malta; National Library of Wales; National Maritime Museum; National Monuments Record Centres (Aberystwyth and Swindon); National Museums and Galleries (Cardiff); National Portrait Gallery (London); National Railway Museum (York); Norfolk Libraries; Order of St. John Museum and Library; Phillips (London); Portsmouth Museums and Records Service; Public Record Office; Regimental Headquarters The Royal Highland Fusiliers (Glasgow); Regimental Museum, The Highlanders (Seaforth, Gordons and Camerons); Royal Commission on Historical Manuscripts; Royal Commission on Ancient and Historical Monuments, Scotland; RCAHM Wales; Royal Geographical Society; Royal Horticultural Society; Royal Institute of British Architects; Royal Naval Museum (Portsmouth); Scottish National Portrait Gallery; Scottish Record Office (Edinburgh); Society of Antiquaries (London); Society of

Merchant Venturers (Bristol); Sothebys (London); South African Library (Cape Town); Southampton City Art Gallery; Swansea Local Studies Librarian; Diana Taylor; Mr. E. Thomas (Pyle); U.S. National Archives (College Park, Maryland); University of Cape Town; Vale of Glamorgan Libraries; Victoria and Albert Museum; Neil Walklate (Cowbridge); Welsh Office; West Glamorgan Archive Service; Wolverhampton Local Studies Library.

Every effort has been made to trace copyright-holders and obtain permission for the use of material. Any omission brought to our attention will be remedied in future editions.

COTTRELL

Contents

Foreword	V
Acknowledgements	VI
List of black and white illustrations	X
List of colour plates	XI

Chapter 1	*Cottrell*	13
Chapter 2	*Merrick*	17
Chapter 3	*Button*	27
Chapter 4	*Gwinnett*	51
Chapter 5	*Earl of Clarendon*	69
Chapter 6	*Tyler*	75
Chapter 7	*Mackintosh*	101
Chapter 8	*William Powell and Sons*	119

Appendix: Owners of Cottrell from 1546	125
Sources	125

COTTRELL

List of Illustrations

Black and White

	Page number
Cottrell from the air	12
Map: archaeological features of Cottrell Park	13
An aerial photograph of the site of Cottrell House, taken in 1977 *(Cambridge University Collection of Air Photographs)*	14
Cottrell Castle Mound *(Royal Commission on the Ancient and Historical Monuments of Wales)*	15
William Herbert, 1st Earl of Pembroke *(National Library of Wales)*	20
John Speed's map of Glamorganshire, 1610 *(National Library of Wales)*	21
Cardiff, from John Speed's map *(National Library of Wales)*	22
Llandaff, from John Speed's map *(National Library of Wales)*	23
Memorial panel to Sir Edward and Lady Stradling, 1590 *(National Museum of Wales and Llantwit Major Parish Council)*	24
"Great Brittaine's Noble and Worthy Councell of Warr", 1624 *(Society of Antiquaries)*	35
Samuel Gwinnett's bookplate *(Thomas Lloyd)*	52
Advertisements from the *Georgia Gazette*, 1765 and 1766	59
A silhouette of Emilia Gwinnett	61
Penlline Castle, 1786 *(National Library of Wales)*	62
Emilia Gwinnett's bookplate *(Thomas Lloyd)*	65
Cottrell House in the early nineteenth century *(Mr. and Mrs. Murray McLaggan)*	72
Admiral Sir Charles Tyler *(Museum of Welsh Life)*	77
Lady Tyler *(Museum of Welsh Life)*	83
"The inshore blockading squadron at Cadiz, July 1797" by Thomas Buttersworth *(National Maritime Museum London)*	85
"The Battery, Portsmouth" by Edward William Cooke *(National Maritime Museum)*	90
Sir George Tyler's bookplate *(Thomas Lloyd)*	93
Cottrell House in the late nineteenth century *(Museum of Welsh Life)*	99
Moy Hall, Inverness-shire, in about 1899 *(RCAHM for Scotland)*	103
The Glamorganshire Hunt at Cottrell, 1901 *(Glamorgan Record Office)*	106
King, Prime Minister and Mackintosh at Moy, 1921	110
Cottrell House in the 1930's	101, 111, 112
Cottrell Interiors, 1930's	113
The Mackintoshes, 1930's	114
Queen Mary at Cottrell, 1938 *(Museum of Welsh Life)*	115
The sale particulars, 1942	116
Summary of lots, 1942	117
The estate, as let, 1942	118
The SS Hillglade unloading at Cardiff	119

COTTRELL

	Page number
A decorated Van	120
The Cumberland discharging butter	120
Neville Johns-Powell and friends	120
John Peel's hunting horn	120
194 Borough High Street, Southwark	121
Clanyon on the way to victory	122
Cottrell House from the air, 1967	123
The golf courses under construction	124
The first drive	124

Colour Plates

"HMS Warrior off the mouth of the river Tagus" by Thomas Buttersworth (National Maritime Museum London)	Cover
Sir Thomas Button, painted in about 1610. Artist unknown (Phillips)	33
Arms of the Merrick family	36
Arms of the Button family	36
"Englishmen in a skirmish with Eskimos" by John White (The British Library)	37
"An English privateer off La Rochelle" by Cornelius Claesz van Wieringen (National Maritime Museum London)	40
"HMS Prince Royal and other shipping in an estuary", by Adam Willaerts (National Maritime Museum London)	41
"An English brig with captured American vessels" by Francis Holman (National Maritime Museum London)	41
Fort William, Calcutta (The British Library)	44
"Portrait of George Venables Vernon" by Thomas Gainsborough (1727 - 1788) (Southampton City Art Gallery and Bridgeman Art Library)	45
"The battle of Copenhagen, 2 April 1801" by Robert Dodd (National Maritime Museum London)	48
Arms of the Gwinnett family	66
Arms of the Tyler family	66
Arms of The Mackintosh	66
"Chatham Dockyard" by Joseph Farington (National Maritime Museum London)	67
"HMS Hydra at Cape Bagur, 7 August 1807" (National Maritime Museum London)	70
Thomas Villiers, second Earl of Clarendon (Hatfield House)	71
"The battle of Trafalgar, 21 October 1805: beginning of the action" by Thomas Buttersworth (National Maritime Museum London)	74
"The fall of Nelson" by Denis Dighton (National Maritime Museum London)	74
Fort Charlotte, St. Vincent: a hand-coloured woodcut of about 1890	78
A map of the Cottrell estate, from the sale particulars of 1942	79

COTTRELL

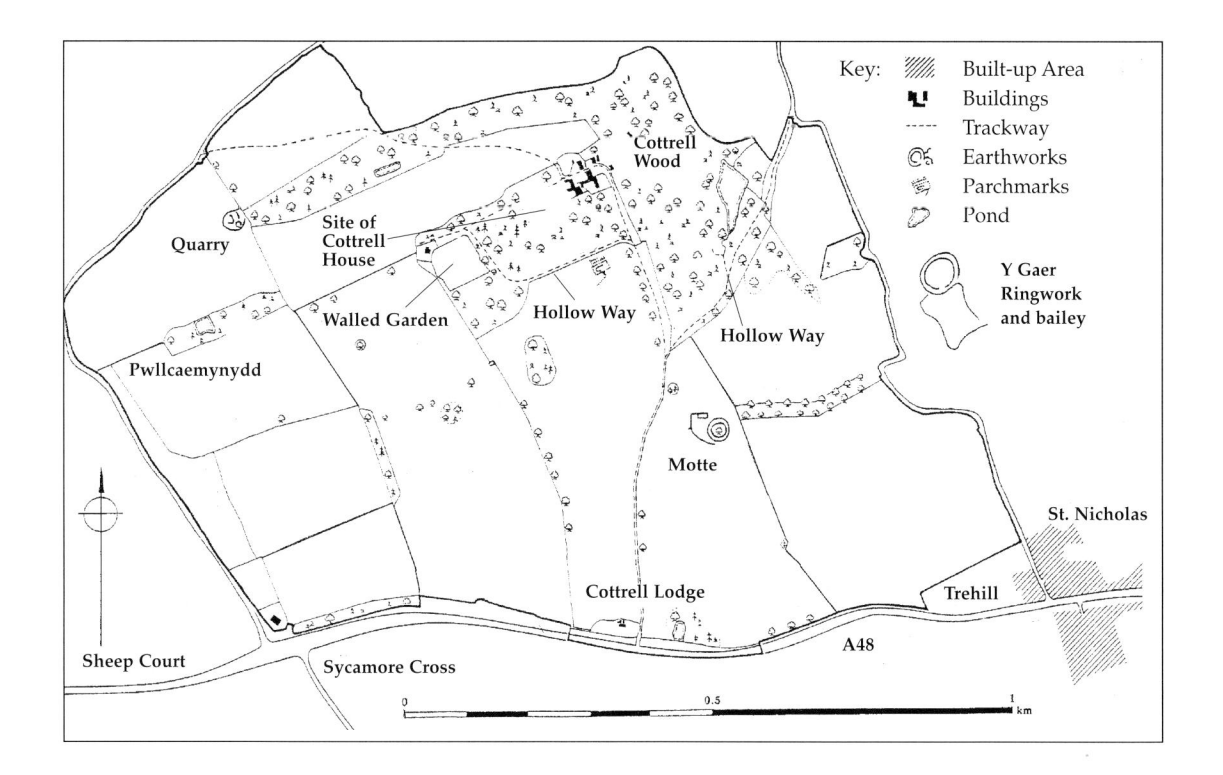

1. Cottrell

ABOVE:
Archaeological features of Cottrell Park.

OPPOSITE:
Cottrell Park in its rural setting, with Peterston-super-Ely at the top and Gwern-y-Steeple in the centre. This aerial view was taken in the 1960s. The area outlined coincides with the map shown above.

Cottrell Park lies halfway between Cardiff and Cowbridge on the A48 (a Roman road, and the ancient Port Way). As you pass through the entrance gates you see, on the left, a thatched cottage which has stood for over two hundred years; the parkland all around you was laid out at about the same time. The woods ahead were first recorded four hundred years ago. Over on the right, now topped by trees, are the remains of an eight hundred years old castle. This, then, is a historic landscape moulded by men and women over a thousand years.

What do we know about these people?
What kind of society did they live in?
What sort of lives did they lead?

In answering these questions we will meet, among others: an Elizabethan squire, with a passion for family and local history; an explorer of Hudson's Bay who was also a scourge of pirates; men and women who suffered the traumas of civil war; an American revolutionary; and one of Nelson's captains at Trafalgar. Not forgetting an unmarried lady who became - because of an illicit liaison - one of the biggest landowners in the county; and a Scottish clan chief turned property developer.

COTTRELL

An aerial view taken in 1977. The walled garden is easily seen; Cottrell House was situated about halfway up the right-hand side of the photo. Experts are unsure about the "parch marks" in the bottom right corner: were they caused by agricultural activities or are they signs of an earlier Cottrell House?

Cottrell Castle

The Normans seized control of the Vale of Glamorgan around the end of the eleventh century. Robert fitz Hamo - a friend of the king, William Rufus - allowed his friends and supporters to grab what they could and settle, building earthwork castles to protect themselves and their newly acquired land. Each castle was not only a redoubt, a residence, and the administrative centre of their estates, but also a symbol of Norman power and domination.

COTTRELL

Cottrell Castle Mound. This is a scheduled "ancient monument" dating from the twelfth century and is, perhaps, the first "Cottrell House". It is a Norman motte originally topped by a timber tower. Associated with the motte was a fortified enclosure providing shelter for people and animals, and storehouses for food.

There are three such castles around the village of St. Nicholas: Y Gaer, Coed-y-Cwm, and Cottrell. The lordship of St. Nicholas was divided into three knight's fees (sub-manors) and it is likely that each of the castles was the strong point of one of these. Cottrell Castle motte, dating from the twelfth century, is a scheduled ancient monument. A *"motte"* is a flat-topped, steep-sided earth mound on which was built a timber tower. Around it was a bailey (a fortified enclosure) in which there were stables, barns, storehouses and living quarters. In times of danger everyone would seek refuge in the tower.

The name **Cottrell** derives from the family associated with the estate in the fourteenth century, and probably from much earlier: the Despenser survey (made for the tax man) shows that Roger Cottrell possessed about 200 acres in the year 1320. Little is known of the Cottrells, and it is with the Merricks that we can begin to see the estate, and the people, more clearly.

COTTRELL

MERRICK

Meurig ap Howell
died 1558
|
Rice Merrick
died 1587
|
Morgan Merrick
died 1624
|
Rice Merrick
|
Barbara Merrick
born 1618
= Miles Button

This is not intended to be a complete family tree. It shows (as do the pedigrees later in the book) people who owned, or were closely associated with, Cottrell.

2. Merrick

Meurig ap Howell

The Merrick family acquired Cottrell in 1546, and held on to it for nearly a hundred years during a period of intense social, religious and economic change, including monetary inflation and an expanding population. This was an aggressive and competitive society, with an ambitious, acquisitive, land-owning "gentry" class coming into its own, gaining new members, and establishing a tight grip on the local community.

Wales and the Marches were, in the early sixteenth century, difficult to govern, although Henry VIII made efforts to improve the situation, culminating in the "Acts of Union" of 1536-1543. Legal matters, defence, and keeping the peace were the responsibility of the Council of Wales and the Marches (based in Ludlow) whose Lord President was a sort of Viceroy, or Governor-General. By the Acts of Union: legal proceedings were to be conducted in English and new offices were instituted, including that of Justice of the Peace. These Justices met regularly in Quarter Sessions, which developed into a part-time administrative body for the county. Other changes were set in train, including the abolition of *cyfran* (the Welsh custom by which inherited land was split up): now, in the manner of England, a landowner could expand his estate knowing that he could pass it on, entire, to his heir.

This was the milieu in which the Merricks lived, and successive members of the family took advantage of the prevailing conditions: buying, inheriting and consolidating property, holding local office, and leaving yeoman farmer status behind to become members of the gentry. They were "upwardly-mobile" and their ascent began with Meurig ap Howell, who was of a Welsh family, rooted in the lordship of Miskin; his father was from Llantrisant. In about 1520 Meurig married a daughter of William ap John of Bonvilston, and moved to his bride's village, being described in a deed of 1528 as a *"freeholder of Bonvilston"*. During the 1540s, he set about increasing his land holdings. In 1543, he paid £46 for land in St. Nicholas and bought more two years later, this time in St. Fagans, for just under £42. His most significant purchase was to come in 1546 when he obtained Cottrell (and the manor of Trehill) which was, in due time, inherited by his son, Rice.

Rice Merrick

First, we have to decide what to call him: Rys Meurig, Rhys Amheurig, Rice Meyricke - his name was spelled in several different ways. As for his first name, there was a fashion at this time for changing the Welsh *Rhys* into the English *Rice* and today he is usually known as "Rice Merrick".

Born in Bonvilston, probably about 1520, he built on the foundations laid by his father, and advanced the status of his family: through property acquisition and management, gaining shire office, scholarship, and by marriage to Mary, daughter of Christopher and Elizabeth Fleming. The Flemings claimed descent from John Fleming, one of those who arrived with the Norman Robert fitz Hamo. More important than this was the fact that Rice's mother-in-law was born a Mansel, being a niece of Sir Rice Mansel of Margam, and cousin of Sir Edward Mansel. This was an age when patronage was of the highest importance - it was difficult to advance in society, in trade or in a profession, without "connections". Progress depended on "who you knew" or, more importantly, who you were related to, however distantly. Rice Merrick's marriage into the powerful and wealthy Mansel clan was thus no hindrance to his family's progress.

In 1550, Rice was still living in Bonvilston, but by 1554 had moved to Pencoed House (now near Capel Llanilltern service area on the M4) where he lived until he inherited Cottrell at around the time of Queen Elizabeth's accession (1558). The second half of the sixteenth century was a boom time for house-building. Many people, then as now, looked on their house as a symbol of their position in society. Most families lived, as they had for generations, in one room: earth-floored, dark and unhealthy. The better-off men now began to think that they needed something better, an imposing residence to emphasize their place in the pecking-order, and many large houses began to appear across the landscape. They let in more light, were more comfortable, and provided greater privacy than the older buildings. The Merricks followed this trend and some time in the late 1550s or early 1560s erected a new house near to what was left of an older structure. Rice Merrick recorded that:

> *The house of Cottrell, sometime lordship of Trehill, called thereof* **Cottrell Court,** *is also decayed, so that the foundations of the old building scarce appear.*

In 1574, Rice bought land in Bonvilston from William Bassett of Beaupré. Before the dissolution of the monasteries, it had belonged to Margam Abbey, and consisted of 441 acres along with houses, cottages and gardens. A deed of 1576 describes Rice Merrick's property portfolio: 24 dwellings, 40 orchards and gardens, 200 acres of arable, 160 acres of meadow, 200 of pasture, 40 of woods and 20 acres of thicket and heath. Of these Rice kept 173 acres in his own hands, probably for mixed farming, including barley. The rest provided income from rents.

Two sixteenth century deeds mention *"Parke mawr"* and *"Parke bach"*- the big park and the little park. This may be a reference to deer parks, where the animals were kept for hunting and as a source of fresh meat. Because deer are great jumpers, a very high boundary was needed, often an earth bank with a wooden palisade or a stone wall on top. Parks were regarded as a sign of the owner's status but most fell into disuse - the costs (including maintenance, feed for the deer, and keepers' wages) making them uneconomic. Rice was to record that his land had been "disparked".

By now Rice Merrick was a substantial landowner and was able to pass on to his son: most of Bonvilston, the western part of St. Nicholas and property in Llancarfan and Pendoylan. He was, we may assume, an effective manager because he was asked to help run the manor of Glynrhondda - in 1583 he was deputy steward to William Mathew and, in 1585, to George Herbert.

The law provided another avenue for advancement. Rice Merrick became an attorney (not unlike a solicitor today) and the Acts of Union proved to be a godsend to anyone with legal training. The key people in the administration of the new shires were the Justices of the Peace, and there was considerable wheeling and dealing to get appointed. The justices were presided over by the *"Custos Rotulorum"* (Keeper of

BELOW:
William Herbert, first Earl of Pembroke. Patron of Rice Merrick, to whom he gave the post of Clerk of the Peace.

the Rolls, or records), an appointment taken by the most influential landowner. The Custos was helped in his duties by the Clerk of the Peace - a post given to Rice Merrick by William Herbert (1st Earl of Pembroke) and again by Henry Herbert (2nd Earl).

These were powerful patrons indeed. Apart from their involvement in court and national affairs, various Herberts were established in Glamorgan at Cardiff, Cogan Pill, Neath and Swansea. The family dominated Welsh politics over a long period and Rice, with such men behind him, was in a fortunate situation, although it has to be said that his Mansel kinsfolk did not always see eye-to-eye with the Herberts. (There was intense rivalry between prominent families, and there were many brawls between gangs of their retainers and supporters).

A Book of the Antiquities of Glamorganshire

Rice Merrick is remembered today not as a landowner or lawyer, but as an antiquarian and author. The sixteenth century saw the

"The shire of Glamorgan... is the southerliest part of all Wales. Far of the south it bordereth on Severn Sea... of the north it pointeth to the mears and confines of Brecknock; on the east part it is separated from Monmouthshire by the river of Rhymni, and in the west it severeth from Carmarthenshire by the river of Loughor"
(Rice Merrick).

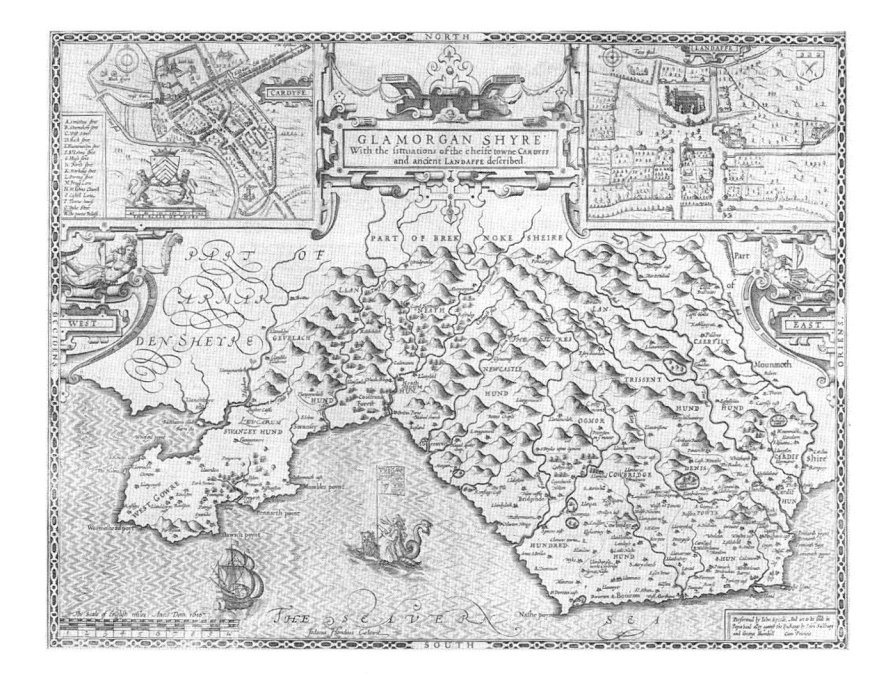

development of a curiosity about the past and about the landscape. Some people began to question Francis Bacon's assertion that "the most ancient times (except what is preserved of them in scriptures) are buried in silence and oblivion". Descriptions of "monuments" began to appear and Henry VIII appointed John Leland as his "antiquary". In 1586 came the publication of William Camden's **Britannia**, providing the first widely-available account of antiquities such as Hadrian's Wall and Stonehenge. Camden described his studies as being motivated by a "back-looking curiositie", and a similar impulse in Wales produced antiquarian and genealogical works by, among others: David Powell of Ruthin, Humphrey Llwyd of Denbigh, George Owen of Henllys, Sir John Wynn of Gwydir, Sir Edward Stradling of St. Donats, and Rice Merrick of Cottrell.

Printed books were becoming easier to get hold of, but work continued to be circulated in manuscript form - borrowed and copied by other interested gentry. Rice Merrick's writings became known in this fashion, and he produced a work on Wales and one on the bishopric of Llandaff, before he compiled his famous **Morganiae Archaiographia: A Book of the Antiquities of Glamorganshire.** It was written around 1580, but the original is lost. There are three copies in existence, all made between 1660 and 1680: Cardiff Central Library has one as do The Queen's College, Oxford, and the National Library of Wales. (An excellent modern version is that edited by Brian Ll. James in 1983.) The manuscript provides a history of the county, and a description of it as it was in the author's time telling us, for example,

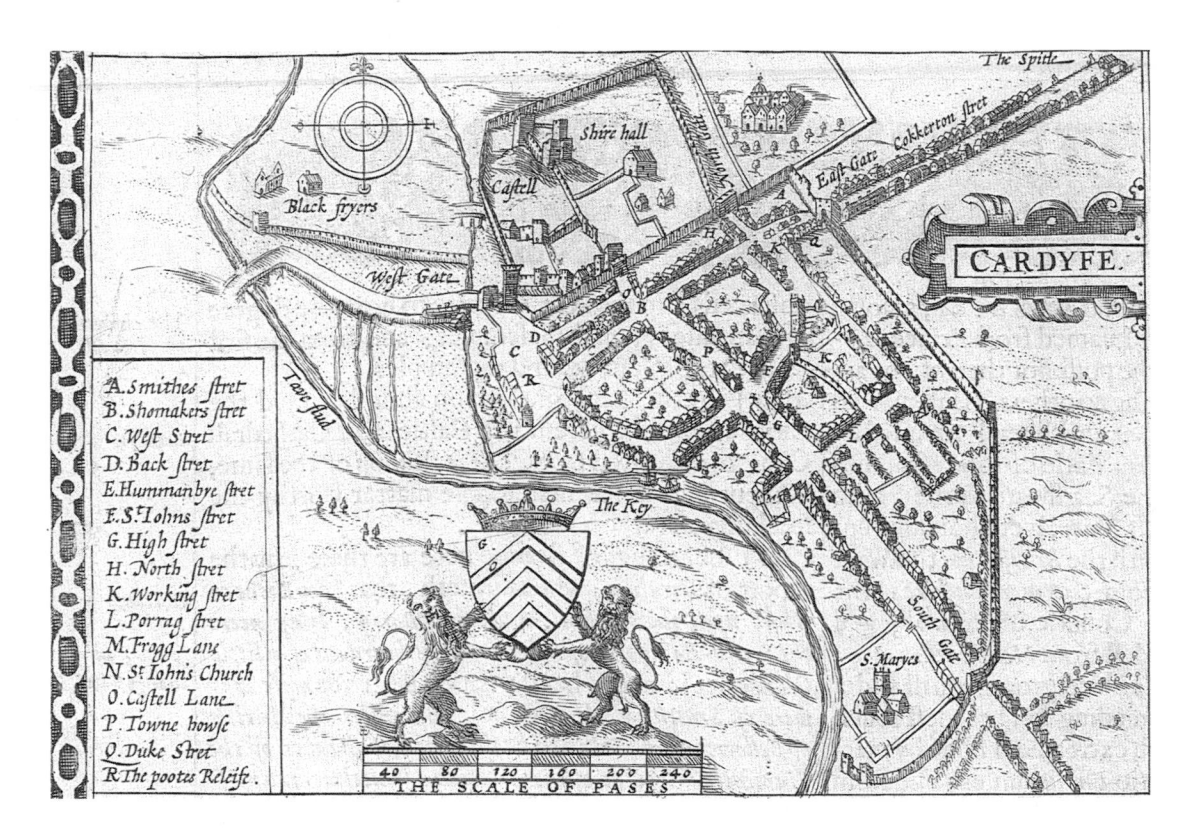

Map key (left side):
- A. Smithes stret
- B. Shomakers stret
- C. West Stret
- D. Back stret
- E. Hummanbye stret
- F. S.t Iohns stret
- G. High stret
- H. North stret
- K. Working stret
- L. Porrag stret
- M. Frogg Lane
- N. St Iohn's Church
- O. Castell Lane
- P. Towne howse
- Q. Duke Stret
- R. The pootes Releife

Cardiff: "The river Taff runneth near the town walls in the west part of the town, and washeth the wall, but somewhat too hard, for part of it is thereby overturned, and the sea floweth to the walls where, at the west angle, is a fair quay ... The town is very well compacted, beautified with many fair houses and large streets; it is almost square or quadrant, but more in length from the south to the north than the other way"
(Rice Merrick).

about the castles, rivers, bridges, markets, estates, towns and villages.

A prime influence on Rice Merrick's work was William Lambarde's **A Perambulation of Kent** (1576) which may be looked on as the first "county history" although its main purpose was to provide a contemporary description of his county. Lambarde hoped that a similar publication could be produced for all other counties, and Rice Merrick was one of the first to respond. In preparing his manuscript he was fortunate in having at St. Donats, close at hand, Sir Edward Stradling's famous library. Rice borrowed (and made extensive use of) Sir Edward's **The Winning of Glamorgan,** a not entirely accurate account of the county's history. Rice returned the manuscript on 18th December 1574:

> *Herein-closed I send your worship's book, wherein the state of Glamorgan for a long time is preserved from oblivion ...I crave the loan of the **Register of Neath Abbey**... and it shall be carefully kept and sent home at your pre-fixed time.*

Apart from **The Winning of Glamorgan** and the **Register of Neath Abbey**, Rice Merrick consulted the **Llandaff Book** *(Liber Landavensis)* which he called "Teilo's Book"- a collection of charters, some of them of doubtful authenticity, and other documents; **Y Cwta Cyfarwydd** (a collection of manuscripts in English, Latin and Welsh

MERRICK

BELOW:
"Llandaff, so named of the river Taff running by, is an ancient city ... In it standeth one fair great church, commonly called Eglwys Teilo, being the cathedral church of that diocese. An old castle standeth in it, sometime the palace of the bishops thereof. And now William Mathew repaireth it"
(Rice Merrick).

dating from the early fifteenth century); and **Llyfr Coch Hergest** (the "Red Book of Hergest" of around 1400). As Clerk of the Peace, Rice also had access to such county records as existed.

It seems likely that Rice's interest in Glamorgan's history and topography sprang out of his genealogical studies. Like many Elizabethan squires he was interested in his ancestors, and those of neighbouring families. He made a large collection of pedigrees, which became known as **The Cottrell Book,** and was regarded as an expert in this field, particularly by the bards who came to consult him. Such a source of information was invaluable to these itinerants, because of the content of the verse to be declaimed: an important element was praise of the poet's patron. As well as enthusing about the attributes of the patron, his house and his generous hospitality, it was essential to rehearse the host's long and, of course, distinguished lineage - not forgetting that of his wife. This was an aspect of the bard's performance that the "new" gentry found particularly gratifying. To be able to consult Rice Merrick's Cottrell Book was thus of enormous benefit to any bard who wanted to check up on a future host's forebears. Dafydd Benwyn and Sion ap Sion are two who are known

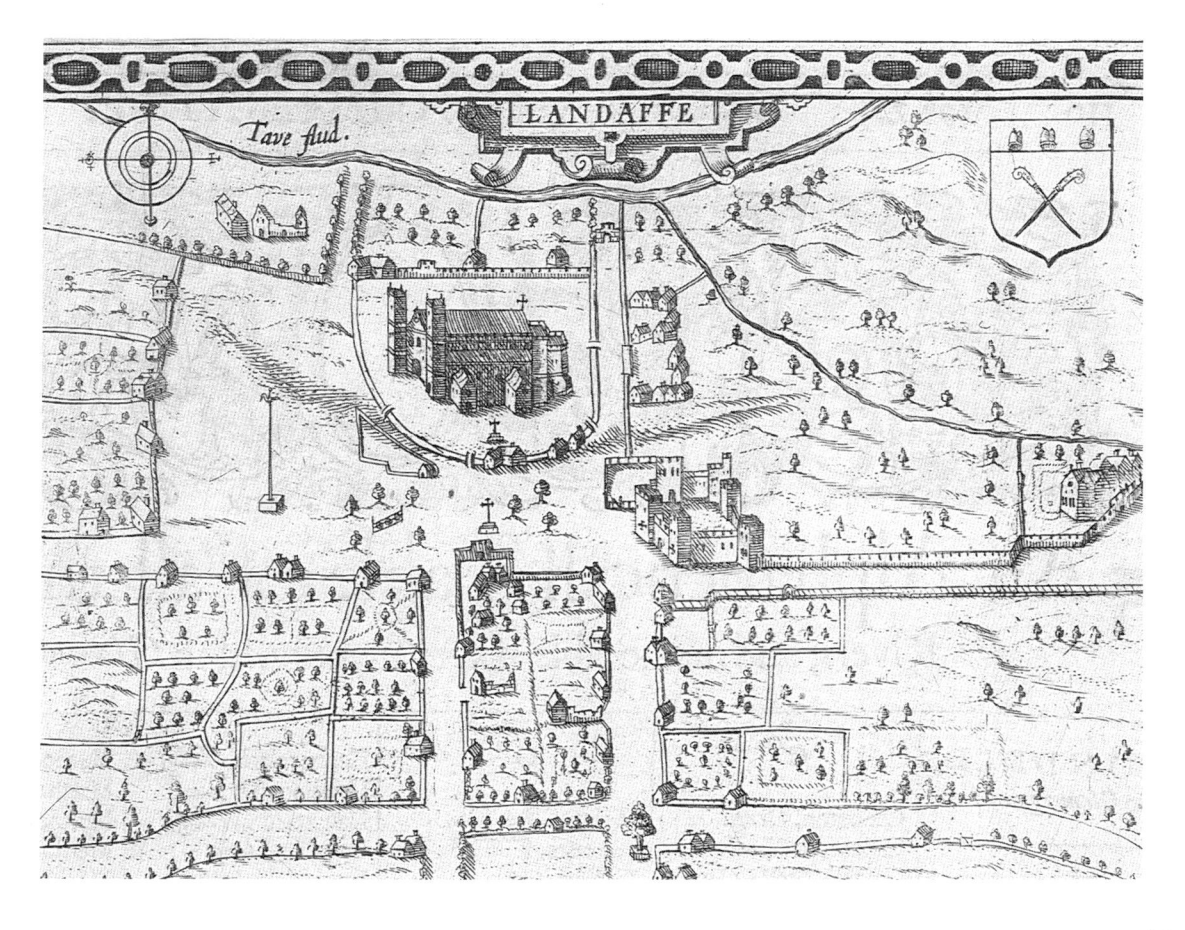

Sir Edward Stradling (1529-1609) placed three commemorative panels in St. Donats church in 1590. This one shows Sir Edward and his wife Agnes. Among his friends were Francis Drake, Richard Grenville, Humphrey Gilbert and Walter Raleigh - seaferers all. Manuscripts from Sir Edward's famous library were borrowed by Rice Merrick to aid his own researches. Rice wrote this tribute: "You refuse things which others most fervently crave and desire viz. gains and profit ... in respect of the zeal ye bear to the public commodity of your country before your own private wealth".

to have come to Cottrell for advice.

The poetry was in the Welsh language, spoken by nearly everyone who lived in Glamorgan. The gentry played an important role in preserving this Welsh poetic activity: in Glamorgan such bards as Lewys Dwnn, Sils ap Sion, Llywellyn Sion, Dafydd Benwyn and Dafydd Meurig were supported by the families of Herbert (Cardiff), Lewis (Y Fan), Stradling (St. Donats), Kemeys (Cefn Mabli) and Mathew (Llandaff). The Cottrell family was well-known for its patronage. Lewis Dwnn - a celebrated genealogist, indebted to the Cottrell manuscripts - made several references to Rice Merrick's collection and praised his learning, as in the *englyn*:

MERRICK

Glain dysg, glain addysg, glan wyd, - Rys Meurug,
Mawredd Cymru'th wraethpwyd,
Gwr odiaeth, gorau ydwyd,
Grym yr iaith a'c gramer wyd.

(The bard praises Rice Merrick for his learning, character, and his fame throughout Wales for encouraging the use of the language.)

Rice Merrick died, in his sixties, on 1st March 1587, two years before his wife, and was buried in the church of St. Nicholas. Eulogies were composed by Dafydd Benwyn and Sils ap Sion, who is broken-hearted at the passing of a man who has been such a friend to the wandering poets:

Ba wiw i feirddion dorri calonnau
Yma fynychu i'mofyn achau.

The tradition continued: fourteen years later, Lewis Dwnn was singing the praises of Rice's three sons - Morgan, William and John.

Morgan Merrick

Morgan Merrick carried on the work of his father and grandfather, buying further acreage in Bonvilston and Llantrisant. By the time of his death, in 1624, he was master of 870 acres, orchards, cottages and gardens, a quarry and a mill. His own house was set among gardens and apple orchards. Like his father, Morgan kept about 170 acres to farm himself, growing barley and wheat, and keeping cattle (including oxen) and sheep. Most of his property was let. There exists, for example, a lease dated 1611 for 50 acres in Bonvilston. The land was let for a period of three lives, for which the tenant paid an "entry fee" of £72 and an annual rent of £1.13s.6d. In addition, he had to give Morgan Merrick two capons a year and provide one day's work at harvest time. The property was to be maintained in good repair, and at the end of each life, a *heriot* of the best beast was to be paid to the landlord.

As was expected, Morgan Merrick played his part in county affairs being, at various times, Coroner, Justice of the Peace and, in 1610, Sheriff. The office of Sheriff was an onerous, but prestigious one, filled by a man from one of the big landowning families - another social step up for the Merricks. The appointment, for one year, was made on the recommendation of the Council of Wales and the Marches. As Sheriff, Morgan had many duties: among other tasks, he produced prisoners for trial, organised juries, collected fines, ensured that sentences were carried out, and collected taxes. He could also manipulate election arrangements so that his favoured candidate was successful.

Morgan Merrick's son and heir, another Rice, was sent (as were so many sons of Welsh gentry) to Jesus College, Oxford, as part of his preparation for taking his proper place in Glamorgan "society". This was not to be. Rice died before his father, and so the Cottrell lands passed to Rice's daughter Barbara, on her grandfather Morgan Merrick's death in 1624.

Barbara Merrick

Barbara was only six years old when her grandfather died, so she was made a Ward of the King (James I). Under the feudal system of tenure, land was granted to a tenant by the king, in return for armed service by the tenant, when called upon. The tenant-in-chief, in turn, would call out his sub-tenants. When a minor was due to inherit the property - as in Barbara Merrick's case - he or she became a ward of the king, on the grounds that the heir was too young to undertake the necessary military service. In practice, the military aspect of tenure had withered away, but the king still insisted on control over inheritance. Often the king appointed one of his courtiers as guardian of the ward, which meant that the guardian could, if he wished, exploit the estate to his own advantage until the ward became twenty-one. This was obviously, for the family, an unmitigated disaster. It was possible, however, for family members to buy the wardship from the king, and so prevent someone else getting their hands on the property. A large sum of money had to be found, but the Merricks managed it. The Court of Wards and Liveries determined that:

> *As part of the lands and tenements were held from the King in chief by Knight's services, the said Barbara was the King's ward.*

But, in return for a payment of £300 (a considerable sum, which shows how valuable the estate had become) the wardship was granted to Anne Merrick (Barbara's grandmother), Margaret Kemeys, and two other female relatives. In addition to the lump sum, the family had to pay a rent of £50 a year during Barbara's minority. She was not to become engaged or marry without the consent of the Court. When she did eventually marry it was to a neighbour, Miles Button of Sheep Court, Bonvilston.

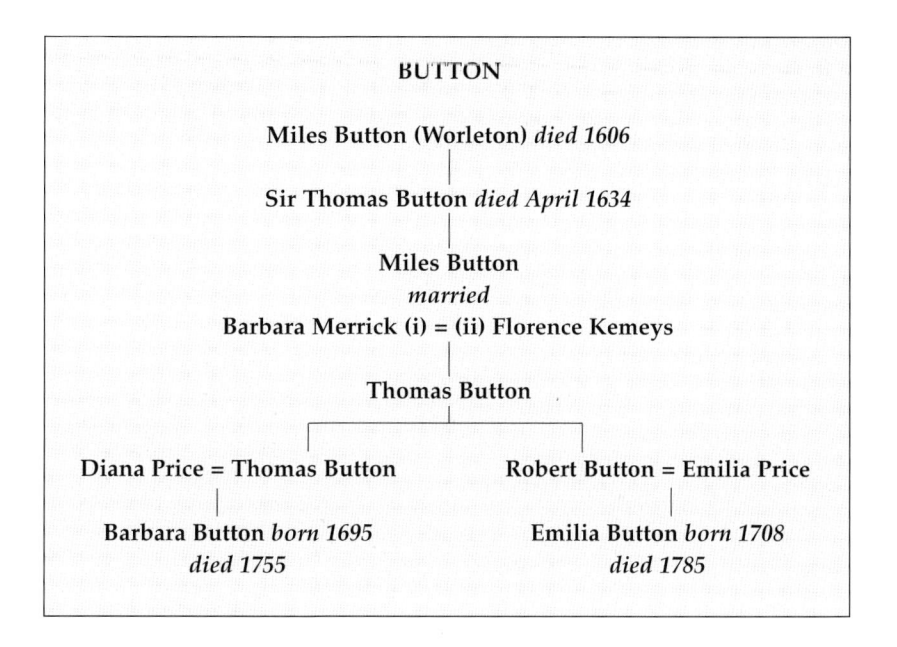

```
                            BUTTON

                   Miles Button (Worleton) died 1606
                                |
                   Sir Thomas Button died April 1634
                                |
                          Miles Button
                            married
               Barbara Merrick (i) = (ii) Florence Kemeys
                                |
                          Thomas Button
                  _____|_____
                 |                             |
    Diana Price = Thomas Button      Robert Button = Emilia Price
                 |                             |
        Barbara Button born 1695      Emilia Button born 1708
                died 1755                  died 1785
```

3. *Button*

Sir Thomas Button

By marrying Barbara Merrick, Miles Button became master of the Cottrell estate, which was to remain in Button hands for nearly a century and a half. The most famous member of the family was Miles's father, Thomas Button - described by a modern naval historian (N.A.M. Rodger) as "one of the most shamelessly corrupt of all the Jacobean admirals". At this time office-holders were unpaid (indeed they often paid to obtain their post) and it was accepted that they would seek to make a profit. The naval world was no exception, from the Lord Admiral downwards. To give one example of how things were done: In 1605 the muster roll of Thomas Button's ship *Answer* (a galleon of 250 tons, with 21 guns) was supposed to have a crew of a hundred men. In reality there were only seventy; the thirty fictitious men were worth four shillings a month to the purser, and six shillings a month to Thomas Button. The depleted crew, of course, had to do the work of the thirty missing men, with inevitable results for the efficiency of the ship. Under these conditions, desertion was common.

There was no permanent fleet recognisable as a 'Royal Navy'. In time of war royal and privately-owned vessels were gathered together:

taking part in the disastrous attack on Cadiz, for example, were fourteen royal and thirty private ships. Men were hired or forced into service as required, and discharged when no longer needed. A seaman's life was rough, hazardous and uncertain, working as opportunity arose in royal service, trading, privateering or even piracy. Thomas Button - fourth son of Miles Button of Worleton - was attracted to such a life, like many another younger son of the Glamorgan squirearchy. (Two of the most famous were Rice Mansel and Robert Mansel to whom Thomas Button was related by marriage.) This was an exciting time to begin a sea-going career: America was being explored and settled by Europeans, Francis Drake had sailed round the world, and Spain's mighty armada had been dispersed in 1588. Under the patronage of Robert Mansel, there were good prospects for young Thomas.

During the year 1601 forces were again being raised to fight against Spain. Thomas Button is to be found in command of the queen's pinnace *Moon*, in action at the siege of Kinsale. Philip II had sent a force of over four thousand men "to deliver Ireland from the jaws of the Devil" but, through bad management and bad luck, they were put ashore at Kinsale, far away from their allies in the north. The Spanish commander, Don Juan del Aquilla, decided to dig in and wait for reinforcements.

Having landed their soldiers the Spanish ships left, leaving the English fleet in control of the harbour. The garrison's supply line was thus severed and, even at this stage, the men lacked equipment, food and clothing. As part of the blockading fleet, Thomas Button and the pinnace *Moon* were stationed in Kinsale Harbour whence he was able to use his guns to bombard the town and prevent troop movements. In December a relieving force appeared, and the besiegers were themselves in danger of bring cut off. The Irish were soon routed and, nine days later, the defenders of Kinsale surrendered. "Thomas Button of Cottrell" was rewarded for his services "on the coast of Ireland" by the grant of a pension of 6s.8d. a day.

Privateering

For some years Thomas Button's main source of income was privateering, that is: as a private venture, attacking the enemy, for profit. In theory, this could be undertaken only to obtain redress for losses sustained by enemy action. A minority of would-be privateers gained their commission (letters patent) directly from the monarch but the more usual method was to make a *querela* (or complaint) to the Lord High Admiral, who could issue a "letter of reprisal". The longer privateering voyages were, usually, undertaken by three or four ships in company and a considerable outlay was needed to prepare them for such a trip. On an expedition to the West Indies, for example, big ships were needed and the men were away for six to nine months. The finance was often beyond the means of one person so there could be two or more joint owners. The crews were not paid a regular wage, but took a share of whatever booty could be found. They were, on the whole, an undisciplined lot - often drunk, violent and quarrelsome.

In the Caribbean, the privateers preyed upon shipping, hoping to seize cargoes of sugar, gold and silver, pearls, wine, indigo or ginger. Captured vessels were sailed home, to be sold as "prizes". People on land were not immune, as the privateer crews attacked and looted villages, farms and sugar plantations. Thomas Button took part in these activities. It is known that in 1602 he commanded the *Wylloby*, which was owned by two other Welshmen: Thomas's relation Sir Robert Mansel, and Sir John Trevor (who was Surveyor of the Navy). The ship arrived home after an absence of more than a year. It was reported, in a private letter to Venice (9 March 1603) that:

> *Captain Newport and Thomas Button together with other men of war took two or three frigates from the West Indies with some three millions of gold and are at Milford Haven, or at some port of Ireland; or in Barbary; however to please the Queen she is made to think it is in a harbour in Wales.*

It sounds as if the captains are covering their tracks and making "adjustments" to their cargo before the queen's officials can make a proper assessment of value! (The Queen was to die a few weeks later, to be succeeded by James I.) Thomas Button had been away so long that his Kinsale pension had been given to someone else and he had to petition to get it restored.

Hudson's Bay

The chief exploit of Thomas Button's life was to be his exploration of Hudson's Bay. The growing trading nations of Britain and Holland were looking to expand their activities in Asia, but the way to the Pacific was barred by the power of Spain and Portugal, so it was necessary to find an alternative route, perhaps to the north of Russia or Canada. Attempts to find a North-West Passage began in 1576 with Martin Frobisher, who lost two of his three ships and had several of his men killed by the Inuit people. The search was continued by John Davies between 1585 and 1587, and by Henry Hudson who sailed *Discovery* into what is now "Hudson's Bay" in 1610. The expedition sat out a severe winter in James Bay and beat off several Inuit attacks. In June 1611 the crew mutinied putting Hudson, his son and seven other men into a boat, and casting them adrift. They were never seen again.

Robert Bylot with great skill and courage brought *Discovery* back to Ireland (Berehaven, Co. Cork) where the half-a-dozen survivors mortgaged the ship for food and passage to England, arriving at Gravesend early in September 1611. Four were put on trial for murder, but acquitted, blaming men now dead for the mutiny. The survivors announced, to everyone's elation, that they had found the North-West Passage. This report generated enormous excitement: it was what seamen and merchants had been longing for. Preparations began, immediately, for another expedition, the command being given to Thomas Button, thanks to his patrons Robert Mansel and John Trevor. A charter was granted by James I to the "Governor and Company of the Merchants of London, Discoverers of the North-West Passage". The members, including Thomas Button, were granted a monopoly of any passage north of 58°, extending to the north or north-west of China or other parts of Asia.

Thomas Button's orders were drawn up by Edward Wright, a mathematician and tutor to Prince Henry, eldest son of the king. Thomas Button's mission was to try to confirm the existence of the North-West Passage. He was to make careful compass observations, but was not to waste time exploring every bay and inlet. He was instructed to take a careful note of the way the tides ran, as an indicator of a possible sea passage. There is no mention in the instructions of any attempt to find poor Henry Hudson and his shipmates.

Resolution and *Discovery* slipped down the Thames in April 1612. (Thomas Button did not tarry for the formal promulgation of the charter, but he was cautious enough to obtain letters patent transferring his pension to his wife, Elizabeth). After an uneventful ocean crossing, the two ships navigated through the Hudson Strait, and into Hudson's Bay - an immense, almost land-locked inland sea, which is covered in pack ice for four or five months of the year. *Resolution* and *Discovery* anchored off Digges Island and stayed for eight days. Captain Hawkridge reported what happened:

> *At Cape Wolstenholme the savages did offer to assault his (Button's) men with two canoes and to the number of seventy or eighty men came upon them until with one musket shot he killed one of their men, and hurt many more when they retired ... sending his pinnace bent on land to take in fresh water, the savages were laid in ambush amongst the rocks and slew him five men dead.*

In the same place, the previous year, four of Hudson's mutineers had been killed.

The two ships journeyed onward and at last saw land: the crews were the first Europeans to cross the Bay and visit the western shore, a region which Thomas Button named *New Wales*. It later became obvious that there was no way out towards a western ocean, so the spot was named *Hopes Checked*. Turning south they followed the coastline; caught in bad weather they were forced to run for shelter to a place which Button named *Port Nelson*, after Robert Nelson (sailing master of the *Resolution*) who died there. Both ships needed urgent repair, winter was coming on, so the men were forced to settle in for an interminable wait until the thaw, suffering from cold, boredom, and sickness. At last, they were able to leave: *Resolution* was abandoned and the weak and weary men sailed on in *Discovery*, still looking for a western passage out of the Bay.

In July 1613, they found themselves back at *Hopes Checked*, convinced by now that there was no North-West Passage through Hudson's Bay. *Discovery* headed for home, appearing in the Thames towards the end of September 1613. Phineas Pett (a member of a famous ship-building family, who had helped Button to choose the vessels for the expedition) noted that:

> *On the 27th September my noble friend, Captain Button, alighted at my door, being newly returned from the dangerous voyage of the North-West Passage, where he had wintered.*

There is still (near Churchill, Manitoba) a Button Bay.

Admiral of the Irish Coast

As a reward for his services, Thomas Button was appointed (in 1613) "Admiral of the King's Ships upon the Coast of Ireland". He was provided with two small vessels and made responsible for a large sea area, including the St. George's and Bristol Channels. The new admiral was supposed to use his miniscule fleet to counter the ever-present menace of attacks by pirates.

From the 1540s onwards pirate vessels wreaked havoc around the coasts of the British Isles. It could be a very profitable activity, often condoned (or even supported with enthusiasm) by those in authority: deputy-lieutenants, vice-admirals, justices, mayors and customs men were all involved. Piracy was rife around Milford Haven, while Cardiff was described as "the general resort of pirates, and there they are sheltered and protected", with a particularly close relationship between some of the local gentry and the pirates. By the time of Thomas Button's appointment the nature of the problem had changed - it was now ships from the Barbary Coast which were the main source of terror for the residents of west Britain. The home bases of the pirates were in north African ports such as Algiers, Bone, Salli (near Rabat), Tripoli and Tunis. These towns were "military republics" which chose their own rulers, and financed themselves by plunder, prizes and people taken into slavery. As the area was under Turkish suzerainty

OPPOSITE:
Sir Thomas Button, painted in about 1610. His chief claim to fame is as an explorer of Hudson's Bay (1612-1613) as part of the quest for the North-West passage. He died in 1634.

(until the middle of the eighteenth century) the pirates were often called "Turks", but they were, frequently, of European origin. Thus, in 1609, the leaders of the Tunisian fleet were Bishop, Ward, and Sir Francis Verney; from Salli, Henry Mainwaring - of a Cheshire gentry family - commanded forty ships and two thousand men, divided into two squadrons under Sir John Fearne and Peter Croston.

It was a vast operation: Algiers alone had a hundred warships (two-thirds of them carrying 25-30 guns), which was far larger than any fleet in Europe. The area of depredation was huge, from Newfoundland to Madeira (1200 people taken in 1617) to Iceland (800 people taken in 1634). To be captured by Barbary pirates was a great evil: men, women and children were treated brutally and sold as slaves. Between 1610 and 1620, twenty-one Bristol ships were captured or plundered by the "Turks". In the years 1625 and 1626 Glamorgan farmers were becoming impoverished by attacks on vessels carrying their butter to France and Ireland. In 1627, Cardiff lost five ships to the Salli pirates.

Thomas Button, with his two small craft, faced a Herculean task. We are fortunate to have an account, by Thomas Button himself, of some of his operations between 1614 and 1622. He provides:

> *A true accounte of services donne by his Majesties shippe the Phenix on the Coaste of Ireland, Under my commaund from July 1614 until this instant January 1622.*

August 1614 He recovered a French ship which had been taken by pirates. The vessel was returned to its owner in Dublin.

September 1614 A pirate, "Captaine Wallsingham" was in Lough Foyle, where his two ships were grounded. Warned of Thomas Button's imminent arrival, he made off, leaving behind one of his vessels (of 60 tons). This was claimed by the Vice-Admiral of Ulster, Lord Chichester.

December 1614 A fleet of ten vessels including *Phoenix* (commanded by Thomas Button) and *Moon* (his old pinnace from the siege of Kinsale) together with two hundred soldiers and artillery pieces were ordered to help put down the Macdonald insurrection by assisting in operations around the Sound of Jura...

> *... where how farre my poor endevors tended to the perfecting of that service (after two monethes miserable endurance in the siedge) I leave to the Relation of Sir Thomas Phillippes, who is now in Towne and best knows it, as allso the then severall Letters of the saide Lorde Chichester both to his majestie and the Lord Sommersett in that behalfe.*

February 1615 Captured Captain Norice, seventy men, his ship (300 tons) and twenty-two pieces of ordinance. Norice and six of his

BUTTON

men were hanged at Cardiff.

In 1616 *Moon* (commanded by Sir Beverley Newcome, serving under Button's command) captured Captain Flemminge, his crew and his ship. Flemminge was hanged in chains at Youghal and many of the crew were executed at Cork in July 1616.

On another occasion:

> Captaine Austins a piratt in a shipp of 100 tonne att Oysterhaven fought with me from 8 in the morninge till 7 att nighte where he and three more of his men were slaine, some drowned, many hurte, his shippe forc'de and buldgde upon the Rockes, the rest of his Company all taken and six of the Chiefest condemned ... in Corcke and so executed. The master allso for example sake (on the head lande nearest the place I tooke them atte) was hanged in chaynes in November 1618.

May 1619 Captain Ellis was hanged at Wapping. Thomas Button captured Ellis, fifty men, their ship (120 tons) and fourteen pieces of ordnance "in the River of Killmarr".

October 1620 Captain Rice (Button's nephew, commanding Button's ship) captured the pirate O'Mally and sixty men, together with their ship and armament. Eight men were killed in the action and twenty-six were hanged at Cork.

> What other services have byn donne by me in the former 23 years of my time spent in the Late Queene and his majesties service (both by the Commissions and Instruction by which I have been employed) (as by other good Testimonies) it shall appeare it hath not been shorte (without disparadgment to any) of any other employed in the same or the like before my time.

The Merchant Venturers of Bristol thought that he was doing a good job, describing him as pre-eminent in trying to suppress "those common enemies of human society the Turkish pirates", even though his ship *Phoenix* had "incurred imminent danger ... for want of men, the coast of Ireland and Channel of Severn being very dangerous in winter time".

In 1620 Sir Robert Mansel was given a fleet and ordered to go to Algiers to confront the pirates at their home port. Sir Richard Hawkins was Vice-Admiral, and Sir Thomas Button (he had been knighted in 1616) was made Rear-Admiral. His ship *Rainbow* (650 tons, 250 men, 40 guns) was part of a flotilla of six royal ships, ten private vessels and two pinnaces. Mansel is usually held responsible for the expedition's lack of success - the pirate base remained untouched - but he had been

BELOW:
A broadsheet depicting the Council of War set up in 1624 to advise King James I on the conduct of the war with Spain.
The members are listed as Oliver, Viscount Grandison; George, Lord Carew; Fulke, Lord Brooke; Arthur, Lord Chichester; Sir Edward Conway; Sir Horace Vere; Sir Edward Cecill; Sir Robert Mansell; Sir John Ogle; Sir Thomas Button.

ordered to use diplomacy rather than force, and not to risk his ships. Only forty British captives were brought home, and the pirates' activities continued as before.

War with Spain 1624-1630

The king set up a Council of War (1624), as a committee of the Privy Council, to advise on the conduct of the war. Sir Thomas Button was made a member, and also appointed to a Commission to "Inquire into the State of the Navy", which meant that he had to spend more time in London. He continued to do battle for money due to him: the Crown still owed him large sums for his services in the late Queen's reign, at least twenty-two years earlier, and he was to spend much of the rest of his life in endless disputes: over the distribution of prize money, his accounting methods, and victualling matters. His vessels were frequently out of commission because of lack of repairs or stores.

COTTRELL

Arms of the Merrick family, owners of Cottrell for over a hundred years, from 1546.

Arms of the Button family.

OPPOSITE:
Attacks by the Inuit were always a hazard in Hudson's Bay. Button's expedition was ambushed at Cape Wolstenholme. Five of his men were killed.

Piratical activities continued unabated: in the year 1626, eighty men of East Looe in Cornwall were abducted. In addition to piracy, the Spanish threat was a continued drain on resources. The Glamorgan justices were ordered to send to Portsmouth, by the end of July "a pinnace or small bark betwixt 30 tonnes and upwards". In 1627 orders were issued for assembling twenty-four archers, together with a further hundred men "of able bodies and yeares, meete for service, and that they shall be well cloathed" to rendezvous at Portsmouth, where six thousand men (mostly pressed and unwilling) were being gathered together for an expedition to La Rochelle. Sir Thomas was ordered to proceed to Portsmouth, with two ships. On the way, both vessels began to leak, and had to seek the shelter of the Scillies. They managed, eventually, to stagger as far as Plymouth, where ships and crews stayed.

May 1628 Sir Thomas was by now back on the Irish Sea, and from now on there are references in his correspondence to the *Lions Whelps*. These were newly-built pinnaces (150 tons, 14 guns), designed for speed and intended for anti-piracy work. (Their name may well have been derived from Psalm 104 where we read of "the whelps of the lions roaring and calling unto god for their meate".) Ten were launched in 1628 and they were, perhaps, the first British ships built as a "class". Unfortunately, they had faults - overloaded with guns, and an inability to sustain long sea patrols "for they spend as they take in victuals and consequently are obliged to hang about the port's mouth for fear of starving". They were too slow to overhaul a pirate frigate. Sir Thomas was allocated two: the *Fifth Whelp* and the *Ninth Whelp*. As well as his duties as Admiral of the Irish Coast, Sir Thomas had other irons in the fire: there are records showing his part-ownership of at least three privateers: *Bonaventure*, *George* and *St. Anne*.

Several of his letters from the following years are extant: he travels between his house at Sandy Haven (Pembrokeshire), Cardiff and London. He takes six days on a stormy passage from Land's End to Ireland. He is ill. His daughter contracts smallpox. He is, to his great satisfaction, consulted by Lord Dorchester about the likelihood of there being a practicable North-West Passage. He replies that:

> *I doe as confidently beleave to be a passadge as I doe there is one either betweene Calis and Dover or betweene holy Head and Ireland.*

The general ineffectiveness of Sir Thomas's Irish Sea flotilla was demonstrated in 1631, when the Dutchman Murat Reis (otherwise Jan Jansz of Haarlem) took away virtually the whole population (120 men, women and children) of Baltimore, County Cork. The *Fifth Whelp* was in Kinsale Harbour immobilised by victualling problems, again (and Sir Thomas himself was near Chester at the time).

36

BUTTON

On 2nd April 1631, Sir Thomas wrote yet again, from Westminster, pleading for the money due to him, otherwise his "wife and seven children must beg". He attends court at Newmarket for twenty-four weeks (in total) in a vain attempt to extract the money. He falls ill on his way home to Wales. The next year (1633) he petitions the King, again to no avail.

By February 1634, his appointment as admiral was under threat. He was summoned to London to answer ten charges of inefficiency, fraud and other misconduct, including failure to prevent the outrage at Baltimore. The case went on through March, with Sir Thomas providing a detailed answer to all the charges. He was not re-appointed - a bitter blow after holding the office for over twenty years. He went home to Glamorgan. A few weeks later he was dead. A friend wrote to the Earl of Strafford, on 1 May 1634:

> *Sir Thomas died of a burning Fever, quickly, much discontented that he lost his Imployment in the Irish Seas.*

Miles Button

Sir Thomas's widow continued trying to extract money from the Exchequer, but with little success. She must, however, have gained some consolation from the marriages made by two of the Button children: Anne, who married Rowland Laugharne from St. Bride's in Pembrokeshire, and Miles who, after his marriage to Barbara Merrick, became owner of the Cottrell estate. He had other property as well, including his father's old house at Sandy Haven - there are documents showing that on 28 October 1641 Miles Button of Cottrell (as owner of the Pembrokeshire house) granted a lease for life to Thomas Stepney for £30 a year. Miles and Barbara had three children (Thomas, Elizabeth and another daughter) before Barbara died, still in her twenties. Miles took as his second wife Florence, daughter of Sir Nicholas Kemeys of Cefn Mabli. Their lives - and those of their family, community and country - were to be turned upside down by the trauma of civil war.

The immediate cause of the war was a dispute over control of the militia. King Charles wanted to raise an army to fight against the Irish but members of parliament (apprehensive that the King might use the army to coerce parliament itself) decided that they would themselves appoint the army's commanders. The King saw this as an unacceptable erosion of his royal prerogative and refused to concede the point. On 5 March 1642 both Houses adopted the *Militia Ordinance,* and ordered its enforcement. This move was opposed in most Welsh counties, and men of influence began to raise money and seize arms and strongpoints, as a precaution.

During the summer it became evident that people, especially the gentry, would have to choose between accepting the authority of the crown or that of parliament. The majority prayed that, if war broke out, it would pass them by, but if their masters took sides they were forced to follow, even though most were completely indifferent; as Lawrence Stone has pointed out "One of the most striking features of the civil war was the almost total passivity of the rural masses". In spite of this, thousands of Welshmen were present, with greater or lesser enthusiasm, on many fields of battle, including the first major one at Edgehill (Warwickshire) on 23 October 1642. In all, about three thousand men lost their lives there, including many from the Vale of Glamorgan. An eye-witness describes the Welsh contingent, led into battle by local magnates such as the Stradlings of St. Donats: "Arms were the great deficiency and the men stood up in the same garments in which they left their native fields, and with scythes, pitchforks and even sickles in their hands".

The following year, after abandoning Sherborne Castle, the Marquis of Hertford arrived in Cardiff, with a small force. He set about raising a new Royalist army and by November 1643 had collected about seven thousand men. Miles Button was at this time a *Commissioner of Array* for Glamorgan, i.e. a member of a committee (of thirty-seven of the county's leading gentry) whose main task was recruiting and raising money for the Royalist cause. Most of the "common people" did not want to join up so impressment was introduced (1644), as was sequestration of the estates of Parliament's supporters.

Miles Button enlisted in the king's cause as an Ensign, but was later gazetted as Lieutenant-Colonel of Foot to his (second) wife's brother, Sir Charles Kemeys, and was with the army of Sir Charles Gerard in 1645. Gerard was a competent, forceful and ruthless soldier, who regained most of south-west Wales for the king, after an uncompromising campaign. In August Gerard and most of his men were recalled because they were needed in England, and the Parliamentary forces swept back again. Many of the early successes for Parliament in Pembrokeshire had been due to Rowland Laugharne (married to Miles Button's sister, Anne). The king's local forces tended to be in dispersed garrisons and their commanders were, on the whole, uninspired, so competent generalship by Rowland Laugharne enabled him to force the surrender of Tenby, Haverfordwest and Milford Haven. Charles Gerard was a different matter altogether and his army (presumably with Miles Button fighting against his brother-in-law) soon had Laugharne boxed up.

It is known that in 1646 Miles Button was in the garrison at Worcester, but his movements over the next two years can only be guessed at. We do know, however, what was happening in the

COTTRELL

BELOW:
Thomas Button's main source of income was from privateering - attacking the enemy for personal profit. The illustration is of an English privateer off La Rochelle in 1616.

countryside around his Cottrell estate during these years - events which had serious effects on both the economy of the estate, and those people still clinging on there. After the royalist defeat at Naseby in June 1645, the king's battered soldiers trudged in retreat to Hereford, but Charles carried on to Cardiff with plans for raising a new force from within Wales. Meeting his Commissioners of Array in Cardiff Castle he demanded one thousand men from each of the counties of Glamorgan and Monmouth; the taxation of Glamorgan was to be raised to £1250 a month. Charles was, however, out of touch - the local Royalist coalition was falling apart and the monarch was faced with fractious and rebellious subjects who were incensed by the depredations of the royal garrisons (scouring the countryside for miles around and commandeering food, animals, crops and anything else that took their fancy) and weary of the blockade by Parliament's ships which had disrupted the local economy.

The Glamorgan men refused to go to war for the king. A worried Charles went to St. Fagans where (July 1645) he was confronted by four thousand armed men led by the local landowners, who wanted to salvage something from the deteriorating situation. They named themselves the *Peaceable Army* and demanded lower taxation and that local gentry should command forces in the county. Under this intense

BUTTON

Ships of Thomas Button's day. Such vessels carried him on the seas of Ireland, Scotland, the Bristol Channel, the West Indies and North America.

Button Gwinnett began trading with the American colonies in the 1750s. He was, for a time, owner of the brig Nancy (similar to the vessel shown here) until it was impounded by bailiffs.

pressure Charles agreed to replace the hated Charles Gerard by Sir Jacob Astley (neither local nor Welsh) and made Sir Richard Bassett of Beaupré governor of Cardiff. The king then departed for England. It was not long before he was back with sufficient force to deal with the Peaceable Army, which was confronted and dispersed. One thousand of its men were immediately conscripted into the king's army.

Almost as soon as the royal warriors left, the Peaceable Army formed up again and declared for Parliament. Bristol was now in Parliament's hands and so troops were available for transfer to Glamorgan, bringing the county firmly under the control of Parliament. Taxation levels (which had been the principal grievance of the Peaceable Army) increased, and puritan religious practices began to be introduced. Within a few months the gentry had had enough and Sir Edward Carne led an armed force to Cardiff, demanding "in the King's name" that the governor surrender. Rowland Laugharne was sent for and his experienced soldiers soon dispersed the dissidents.

The first civil war ended in the next year when Charles surrendered to the Scots and, with the fall of the royalist fortress of Raglan, fighting in south Wales came to an end. Or so it appeared. Less than a year later, trouble flared up again in the Vale of Glamorgan: on 13 June 1647 some of the gentry distributed warrants calling a general muster at Cowbridge. The revolt was set in motion by people like Sir Richard Bassett (the former Royalist governor of Cardiff) and Sir Henry Stradling (formerly governor of Carlisle) who directed their grievances against the Parliamentary County Committee - they charged it with the arbitrary use of power, especially in taxation matters, and corruption. Something like two thousand men turned up and trudged along the Port Way, past Cottrell, towards Cardiff. Rowland Laugharne (called up again to his wife's home area) intervened once more and the rebel band melted away. The leaders fled abroad.

The Second Civil War began in Wales at Pembroke, but culminated, with much blood shed, near to Cottrell. Events turned, initially around John Poyer. (Several authors state that Poyer was married to another of Miles Button's sisters, but there is some doubt about this.)

John Poyer, a local merchant, had held Pembroke Castle throughout the war on Parliament's behalf. When hostilities ended he began to be criticized by some influential local families who accused him of shady financial dealings. He began to believe that his life was in danger. At the same time, Parliament was trying to disband part of its army, including some of the Pembroke garrison (without giving the soldiers the arrears of pay due to them) and send the rest off to Ireland.

Poyer was ordered, as part of a planned programme of handing over fortresses, to deliver the castle up to Colonel Fleming. Poyer refused, demanding an indemnity for himself and payment for his men. From all over west Wales disgruntled soldiers began to converge on Pembroke and, on 10 April 1648, John Poyer declared for the king. Men of Rowland Laugharne's army came in with him as did Rice Powell (Laugharne's deputy) who led an attack on Carmarthen, followed up by the capture of Swansea and Neath.

The men attracted to Powell and Poyer totalled, perhaps, eight thousand but were not likely to be an effective fighting unit. They were a motley lot - disaffected Parliamentarians, Royalists and Presbyterians, many of whom may have been forced to join. Major-General Rowland Laugharne was not with them, but in London. There had, for some time, been rumours that he was involved in Royalist plots, so he was ordered to the capital, not into gaol but free on parole. Learning that Rice Powell and his men were advancing towards Cardiff, Laugharne broke his parole and set off for his brother-in-law Miles Button's house of Cottrell, arriving on 4 May 1648.

The government had, obviously, been following events in west Wales with growing alarm and dispatched a force under Colonel Thomas Horton, a very experienced and capable commander. At Brecon, en route to Pembrokeshire, Horton learned of the threat to Cardiff and altered his plans accordingly. Writing to General Fairfax, Horton reported:

> *We were necessitated for the preservation of (Cardiff) and prevention of the enemies' design of entirely raising the Counties of Glamorgan and Monmouth ... to march with all possible speed towards Cardiff, which was done with much difficulty, by reason of all the ways being over mountains, very unseasonable weather, and want of accommodations both for horse and man. At last we passed the River Taff, at Llandaff, about a mile above Cardiff, and came to St. Fagans, upon the River Ely ... (the enemy being) at St. Nicholas, two miles from us on the other side of the River Ely, being a place much to their advantage, where we could make no use of our horse and because, for want of food, we could not rationally attempt anything upon them.*

He states that south Wales "is generally against the Parliament" so his force is operating in hostile territory.

The Welsh troops were now centred on Cottrell, and disposed in the villages round about, including St. Hilary, Bonvilston, Llancarfan, Penmark, and at Fonmon Castle. Most were sleeping rough in the sodden, muddy fields, with a lucky few commandeering barns and

COTTRELL

Fort William, Calcutta, as it looked at the time of John Gwinnett's arrival. In March 1773 he was given command of a locally-raised battalion, but died six months later.

OPPOSITE:
George Venables Vernon. His wife cut him out of her will because of his infidelity (particularly with their daughter's maidservant). Lady Vernon bequeathed Penlline Castle to her friend Emilia Gwinnett, of Cottrell.

houses. As with Horton's force, food and fodder was almost non-existent. Rowland Laugharne (with considerable chutzpah) decided to write to Thomas Horton questioning his authority:

> I desire you would let me know by what power you came and still remain in these counties of my association, I being commissioned Commander-in-Chief in these parts by an Ordinance of Parliament.

Horton replied that he came on the direct orders of General Fairfax, who commanded all Parliamentary forces. He expressed astonishment that Laugharne should join those "who have so manifestly violated the authority of Parliament".

The stage was thus set for the battle of St. Fagans, generally reckoned to be the biggest civil war battle in Wales. What we know of

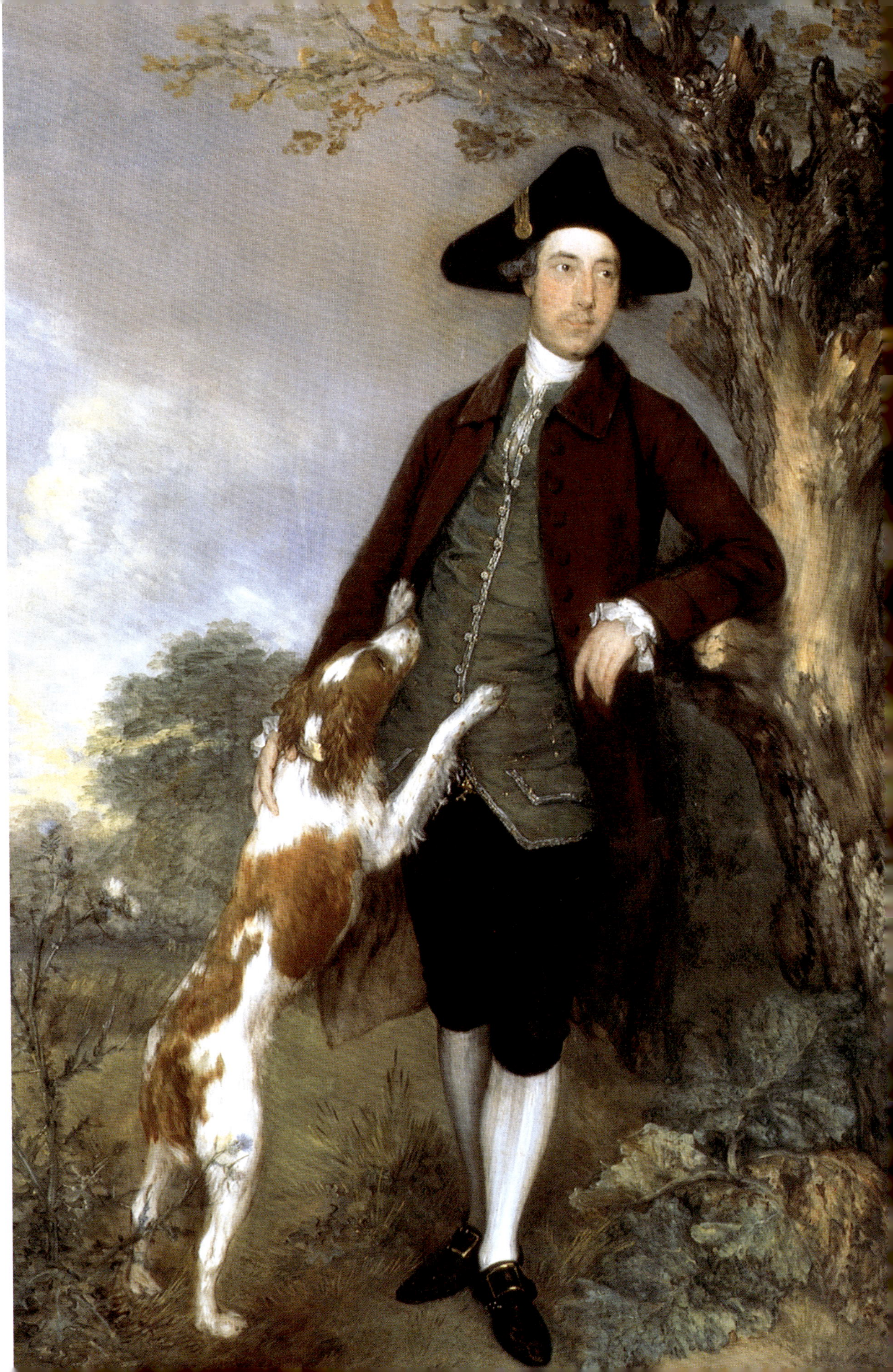

it comes from the Royalist side only, in particular Horton's dispatch to Fairfax, sent from Bridgend on 13 May 1648. Parliament's order of battle consisted of about three thousand well-equipped men, with the cavalry stationed on each wing, and the foot-soldiers in the centre. The whole array was about a mile long and lay across the St. Brides to Fairwater road.

The Welsh, about eight thousand strong, began their advance from Cottrell in the early morning of 8 May. There were many local landowners among them, including three Stradlings. Miles Button was accompanied by his wife's brother (Sir Charles Kemeys) and his sister's husband (Rowland Laugharne, the Commanding General) now facing his former Parliament comrades-in-arms. It was a grim struggle, over about two hours, in which Parliament's trained and battle-hardened infantry, aided at crucial times by cavalry, and skilfully commanded, gradually prevailed. Horton lost very few men, the Welsh about two hundred dead with over three thousand taken prisoner, including John Stradling who was to die as a prisoner in Windsor Castle. Three officer prisoners were put to death and 240 of the "bachelors" were sold, for one shilling each, to be transported to Barbados. (The economy of the island of Barbados was then being transformed by the development of sugar plantations; there was a severe labour shortage and criminals and political offenders were often sent there. This process was known in seventeenth century Britain as being "Barbadosed".)

A hundred and fifty years later, during the drainage of a field at Whitton Mawr, large numbers of skulls and bones were found. The Reverend J.M. Treharne believed them to be the remains of Welsh soldiers, fleeing from St. Fagans. Most of the survivors went home. Some, especially the leaders, struggled back to west Wales, seeking the sanctuary of Pembroke and Tenby. Oliver Cromwell, meanwhile, was on his way with a large army from London, passing through Cardiff on 15 May and arriving at Tenby on 23rd. Leaving the siege of Tenby in Thomas Horton's hands, Cromwell went on to invest Pembroke, bombarding the castle into submission. Within its walls Rowland Laugharne, who had been wounded at St. Fagans, was "very sicke of body and minde", so the compassionate Oliver Cromwell allowed Anne Laugharne into the castle to see her husband, and her brother Miles. (She was allowed to take a doctor with her.) After a stubborn resistance, the end came on 31st May 1648. Articles of Surrender were drawn up: those "to surrender to the mercy of Parliament" included Major-General Laugharne and Colonel Poyer, while "exiled abroad for two years" were (among others) Mr. Miles Button, Sir Henry Stradling, Thomas Stradling, and Sir Charles Kemeys.

Laugharne, Powell and Poyer were hauled off to imprisonment in

London and, almost a year later, condemned to death by a court martial. Their relatives petitioned for clemency, Anne Laugharne pleading that her husband's single lapse of judgement "might not cause all his former eminent services to be forgotten". The Council of State decided that only one of the three should die, and so Fairfax ordered them to draw lots. The unfortunate John Poyer was shot (at Covent Garden) on 25 May 1649. King Charles II had been beheaded in Whitehall on 30 January. In March, Acts were passed which abolished the House of Lords and the monarchy. In the month of Poyer's death England and Wales were proclaimed a "Commonwealth and free state".

Over the following years, Miles Button must have reflected often upon the damage done to his family by the war. His wife's father, Sir Nicholas Kemeys, was killed in May 1648 defending Chepstow Castle. His wife's brother, Charles Kemeys, was imprisoned in Cardiff until December 1651; he died in 1658. Miles Button's sister, Anne, and her husband Rowland Laugharne were ruined, and spent the rest of their lives in debt. In 1670 Anne wrote that Rowland had been forced "to pawn his cloak and sword and has only three shillings in the world". Apart from constant money worries, there was to be more tragedy: their son, Captain Arthur Laugharne (who served the Royalist cause at sea) died in command of the *Revenge* in 1665. Their grandson, another Arthur, was killed commanding the *Colchester* in a battle with the French. Rowland Laugharne died on 16 November 1675 and was buried at St. Margaret's, Westminster. Anne Laugharne died six years later.

Miles Button's exile was for two years. Meanwhile the Committee for Compounding considered the punishment to be imposed for his "delinquency" in both wars: a survey of the Cottrell estate was made, and its debts and charges listed. This was done by a local committee which passed on its findings to London, where the authorities calculated a fine, expressed as a proportion of the estate's value. A substantial penalty was imposed on Miles, and it is estimated that in all he lost about £5500 in the wars - at a time when his annual income was £400. His rental income must have been severely reduced, as the local economy had been shattered by the conflict. Groups of soldiers - ranging from small groups to large armies - lived "off the country" and trade was badly disrupted, especially with the local metropolis, Bristol. The effects on the people in and around Cottrell were catastrophic: forced into fighting, under-nourished, and having to live with the possibility of maiming or death. Many poor families were devastated by the loss of husbands, fathers or brothers, and ruined by soldiers' thefts of precious food, crops, a pig, or a horse. Speaking in the 1647 Army debates at Putney, Thomas Rainborough

Charles Tyler and Warrior were at Copenhagen in March 1801, but took no part in the destruction of the Danish fleet. The ship had a support role with Sir Hyde Parker's squadron.

reminded the gathering that "the poorest he ... hath a life to live, as the greatest he": the tribulations of the wealthy are well-documented, but the suffering of the *gwerin* should not be forgotten. William Price of Rhiwlas could not forget: it was, he remembered: "A Distempered and Bedlam time".

Thomas Button

The next master of Cottrell was Thomas, son of Miles Button and Barbara (Merrick). Thomas Button married Gwenllian Lewis, daughter of Sir Thomas Lewis of Penmark. Their family tree turned out as shown opposite:

The brothers Thomas and Robert Button married the Price sisters, Diana and Emilia, from Wistaston Court near Hereford. The younger brother, Robert, went to live at Llandough Castle (near Cowbridge) which he rented from Sir Thomas Mansel in 1706. Robert died two years later, a few months after the birth of his daughter, Emilia, who was, eventually, to inherit the Cottrell estates.

Thomas and Diana Button lived at Cottrell with their daughter, Barbara, the likely heiress. It looks as if her father sired a child out of wedlock because Edward Jenkins of Llandough was appointed guardian (4 January 1714) of Miles Button "natural son of Thomas Button of Cottrell". Almost two years later, the boy was articled for three years to Thomas Lyte, a London solicitor.

Barbara Button came into her inheritance in 1718 at the age of twenty-three and was to live at Cottrell for a further thirty-seven years. In the 1730s she had the estate prospected for copper, lead and tin, and also appointed (1720) a young chaplain (Thomas Williams, rector of Michaelston-le-Pit) who was to live at Cottrell for sixteen years. Barbara Button never married and was, perhaps inevitably, the subject of gossip. A decade after her death schoolmaster William Thomas was chatting to "Old Kate", who recalled events of some years before: after dark, William Rosser found a baby on his doorstep. As it was Christmas time, the girl was given the name "Margaret Nicholas" and was to be brought up at the parish expense. She was thought to be the illegitimate child of Miss Button "from the young man of Aberaman". Many years later (1799) the parish register was to record the burial, four days before Christmas, of "Margaret, illegitimate daughter of Thomas Bassett". Could this be "Margaret Nicholas"? (A branch of the Bassett family lived in Aberaman.)

Barbara's Button's will was proved on 24 March 1755: she made bequests to the poor of Bonvilston and St. Nicholas and to various servants including Elizabeth Jones, Mary Morgan and Jennet Rees.

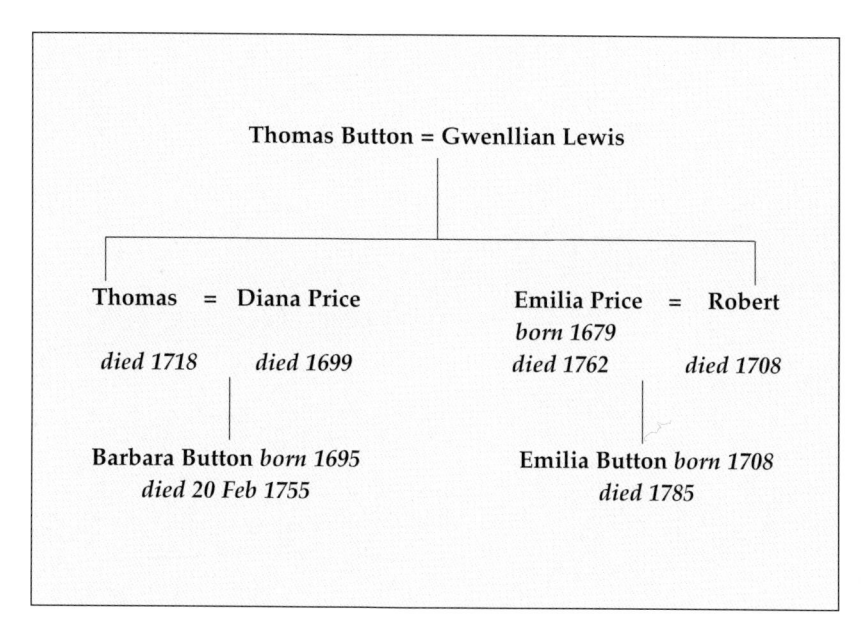

```
                    Thomas Button = Gwenllian Lewis
                              |
          ┌───────────────────┴───────────────────┐
   Thomas   =   Diana Price          Emilia Price   =   Robert
                                     born 1679
   died 1718    died 1699            died 1762          died 1708
        |                                    |
   Barbara Button born 1695          Emilia Button born 1708
       died 20 Feb 1755                  died 1785
```

There were several gifts to the Gwinnett family, but she could not have known that, before long, one of the Gwinnetts would be installed as seigneur of Cottrell. She bequeathed:

To her cousin Anne Gwinnett (wife of Revd. Samuel Gwinnett, senior) £20 to buy mourning clothes, and £30 a year for life;

To Anne and Samuel Gwinnett's children -

Revd. Samuel Gwinnett, junior	£500
Button Gwinnett (Barbara's godson)	£100
John Price Gwinnett	£50
Emilia Gwinnett	£50

To her cousin, Emilia Button, spinster "all and singular of my Manors, messuages, lands, tenements and hereditaments... for and during the term of her natural life".

In other words, Emilia Button, at the age of forty-seven, was suddenly a wealthy woman and heiress of Cottrell.

> **GWINNETT**
>
> The Reverend Samuel Gwinnett married Anne Emes
>
> Three of their children died young:
>
> Anna Maria Gwinnett
> Thomas Price Gwinnett
> Robert Gwinnett
>
> The other children are the main characters in this chapter:
>
> The Reverend Samuel Gwinnett (junior) 1732 -1792
> Button Gwinnett 1735 -1777
> John Price Gwinnett 1737 -1773
> Emilia Gwinnett 1741 -1807

4. Gwinnett

The Reverend Samuel Gwinnett

Barbara Button's will was proved in March 1755 and just over six months later the heiress Emilia Button (aged 47), married the curate of St. Nicholas, Samuel Gwinnett (aged 23). The bride and groom were distantly related. Samuel was to be master of Cottrell for nearly forty years.

The Reverend Samuel Gwinnett's father, also a Reverend Samuel Gwinnett, was Vicar of Down Hatherley, Gloucester. After graduating from Cambridge Samuel Gwinnett (senior) married Anne Emes of Wistaston Court. The Gwinnetts evidently kept in close touch with their richer Button relations - Anna Maria (first child of Sam senior and Anne) - died aged fourteen, whilst staying at Cottrell.

Anna Maria's younger brother, Sam, was aged thirteen when she died. Four years later he was admitted to Oriel College Oxford, where he seems to have developed an inclination towards literary pursuits. Gloucester Library has the manuscript of a play by Samuel called *The Appian Violence: An Historic Piece*. There is also *Lusus Pueriles: or essays in prose and verse,* which include a poem to Miss X of Gloucester and verses dedicated to Dr. Caple. Samuel commented on political events

Samuel Gwinnett's bookplate.

Sam. Gwinnett ex Aul:
B.M. Virg: Oxon

in *On our worthy corporation - Gloucester's pulling down the cross* (1751) and *To Charles Barrow on being elected Member of Parliament* (1754).

Young Samuel had been bequeathed £500 in Barbara Button's will, but was now to gain a much larger prize: the two thousand acres of Cottrell land which, following his marriage to Emilia Button, he was to control for virtually the whole of the second half of the eighteenth century. Bonnie Prince Charlie's rebellion had been crushed barely nine years before; the Seven Years War was to begin in the year following his marriage; George III became king in 1760 and reigned for sixty years, having to cope not only with his porphyria, but also with the effects of the American and French revolutions.

As a *squarson* (both squire **and** parson), Samuel Gwinnett personified one aspect of the social structure of the Vale of Glamorgan. The gentry by now owned most of the land and employed most of the people. To add to their power they had pretty well cornered the ecclesiastical market, with two-thirds of the local parish livings being in the gift of local big-wigs who, of course, found that their own kinsmen were the most suitable candidates. The eldest son was groomed to take over the estate and the younger ones had to make do with a career in the army or the church. There was, nevertheless, some erosion of gentry power in the Vale as they began to be out-ranked by a number of peers who acquired local properties by marrying heiresses. Those arriving on the scene in this way included My Lords Bute, Plymouth, Talbot and Vernon.

As for the less exalted, the diary of William Thomas of Michaelston provides us with an intriguing insight into their lives. He tells us that in 1762 the Vale is still strongly linked to Bristol, which is full of Welshmen. He records, locally, drunkenness and violence and "much noise and swearing and cursing" at cockfights. Horse races on Stalling Down are very popular with "much noise and rioting everywhere". Many died of smallpox (fifty in two months in Cardiff), as a result of childbirth, and of "lingering disease". It was a grim existence in the eighteenth century. Through William Thomas's eyes we may catch a fleeting glimpse of some Cottrell lives, marriages and deaths:

19 September 1763 Barbara Davis was buried at Bonvilston. She was the widow of "Robert of Cottrell, a fiddler" who presumably earned his living by playing at country dances held in local villages. Barbara's death left as orphans six children ranging in age from five to fifteen, the eldest being physically handicapped.

9 November 1765 We learn that Emilia Button (now Mrs Gwinnett) was a "Non-Juror". Mr. Varrior, who was seventy, has been buried at St. Fagans. Like Mrs. Gwinnett, he was a non-juror, that is a successor to those who refused to break their oath to James II and take another to William III in 1688. The non-juror beliefs persisted for many years, with adherents meeting to take the sacrament among themselves. In the Cardiff area the group had almost died out, but Mrs. Gwinnett still kept their chalice at Cottrell.

19 April 1766 Burial of John Thomas, aged about sixty. In his youth his sweetheart (who worked at Cottrell) had given birth to their child, but the pair were so scared that they killed the baby by dropping it down a well. They escaped the noose, were eventually released from gaol, married, and lived exemplary lives thereafter.

August 1768 Samuel Gwinnett's mother died.

3 July 1777 The housekeeper at Cottrell was buried at Pendoylan. Only twenty-nine, she died of "lingering consumption".

12 November 1784 Mary Lewis, a servant at Cottrell, married - as his second wife - John Williams of the Dusty Forge Inn.

2 August 1785 The funeral of Catherine Lewis, a servant at Cottrell. She was aged about forty and her sister (wife of Harry Morgan of the Old Post Inn) had been interred only a fortnight before, in the same churchyard.

20 October 1785 Emilia, wife of the Reverend Samuel Gwinnett, was buried at St. Nicholas. She was seventy-seven and had been married to Sam for thirty years.

23 June 1786 Mr. Howells (the curate of St. Nicholas) married the housekeeper of Cottrell (who was the daughter of the Reverend Mr. Thomas of Bonvilston).

12 December 1791 Buried at Bonvilston: John Williams (see above, 12 November 1784) who was aged forty-eight, and innkeeper of the Dusty Forge. A Carmarthenshire man, he was at one time employed as a servant by Samuel Gwinnett. Mary, his second wife, had died before him. The diarist, William Thomas, had his own views on the cause of John Williams's death: it was because of "weakness of his vitals, weared out by his overmuch drinking".

5 January 1792 Samuel Gwinnett was buried at St. Nicholas. William Thomas described him as being learned in Greek and Latin, but selfish and bad-tempered. "He was rose up a Clergyman but lived a Gentleman, for he married the heiress of Cottrell, his relation... He died 2nd instant of a lingering disease".

John Price Gwinnett

17 January 1763: William Thomas's diary records the funeral of Catherine, housekeeper to the Gwinnetts at Cottrell. Catherine and her sister came from Llandough-juxta-Cowbridge and both girls had been "bred up" by Mrs. Gwinnett. (A few years before, Catherine's sister had given birth to an illegitimate child by William Lucas, Cottrell's Under-Bailiff.) Catherine, unmarried, died in childbirth, after suffering nine days of labour and incompetent midwifery. The still-born child's father was John Price Gwinnett (a younger brother of Samuel) who had been staying at Cottrell. The effects of such a tragedy on the clerical household can be imagined.

Lieutenant John Gwinnett was aged twenty-six and an officer in the 47th Regiment of Foot (later The Loyal North Lancashire Regiment). Not long after Catherine's death he left Britain and joined the East India Company's army in Madras. Before he sailed (the voyage would take at least six months) he made his will, which was very concise and began: "I commend my soul into the hands of Almighty God hoping for remission of all my sins through the merits of Jesus Christ my Lord and Savour". He was well-advised to make a will - in the eighteenth century only about a third of the East India Company's officials survived the ravages of climate, cholera, typhoid and malaria. Famine was a recurring nightmare; in 1769-1770 between one-third and one-fifth of the inhabitants of Bengal died.

After a year in Madras John Gwinnett transferred to the army of Bengal where the Company had won control only recently, through the efforts of Robert Clive who had secured the *diwan* giving the Company the right to collect the revenues. This was enforced by its own army, made up of European mercenaries whose main aim was, of course, to make money. (In 1766 many European officers refused to obey orders, because of a dispute about their allowances.) There were increasing numbers of "sepoys" (locally-raised soldiers - by 1768 about 25,000 of them).

In March 1773, John Gwinnett, now a Captain, was appointed to the post of commanding officer of the 2nd Battalion of Sepoys. shortly after having been refused command of a similar battalion "as he had not long before returned from a visit of some years to Europe".

After 1757 a large garrison was placed in the new Fort William, in the growing city of Calcutta (120,000 people in 1750). The Calcutta John Gwinnett knew was described as "that scattered and confused chaos of houses, huts, sheds, streets and lanes, alleys, windings, gutters, sinks and tanks, which jumbled into an undistinguished mass of corruption equally offensive to human sense and health". John Gwinnett died in September 1773 at Berhampore near Calcutta; he had survived Catherine, the housekeeper, by ten years.

Button Gwinnett

Button Gwinnett, like his brother John, was a rover. Their elder brother, Samuel, stayed put at Cottrell for forty years, but as John Gwinnett was disembarking at Madras, Button Gwinnett was setting up as a trader in Savannah, Georgia.

We know that Button Gwinnett was baptised in St. Catharine's church, Gloucester, was brought up in the vicarage at Down Hatherley, and was left £100 by his godmother, Barbara Button - a relationship which explains his unusual first name. The next twenty years are a blank to us, until we find the record of his marriage - in St. Peter's church, Wolverhampton - to Anne Bourne, daughter of Aaron and Sarah Bourne of Brewood. Button and Anne were to have three daughters: Amelia, Jane and Elizabeth, but only the latter reached adulthood.

The Commercial Button

Wolverhampton at this time was a town of about eight thousand people, and Button appears to have become involved in its commercial life through helping in his father-in-law's business. (Aaron Bourne has been described as a "grocer"; but this term was used interchangeably with "draper" or "mercer" in those days.) Button Gwinnett's uncle was a merchant in Bristol, and is likely to have provided Button's initiation into the business of trading across the Atlantic. Bristol was an important manufacturing centre, processing cotton, tobacco, sugar, chocolate and cocoa. All of these activities developed, of course, because the city was an important port. Its dealings with north America (including a considerable slave trade) were in the hands of about two hundred merchants, who frequently organised themselves into syndicates, so that a ship or cargo might be owned by several people - some, perhaps, with as small a share as three per cent. The goods would be sold at the port of arrival by the ship's captain or, alternatively, a **supercargo** (superintendent of cargo) might make the voyage to be responsible for the business side of the enterprise.

Around 1759, Button Gwinnett began to export on his own account, and to take passage as supercargo. His Wolverhampton family links would certainly have been a help - Midland manufacturers of hardware were eager to make money from the expanding markets of north America and Button Gwinnett could, presumably, obtain suitable goods on credit from his father-in-law and through Aaron Bourne's trade connections. Wolverhampton had become a centre for lock-making, Walsall made spurs, bridles and stirrups while Burslem (only thirty miles away) boasted of a hundred and fifty potteries employing seven thousand people.

Button Gwinnett's trading goods could be taken by road the dozen or so miles to the river port of Bridgnorth. (After 1772 this initial land journey became unnecessary because of the opening of the Staffordshire and Worcestershire canal which joined the Severn at Stourport, the first canal town.) Passenger wherries ran to a timetable down the Severn to Gloucester, and cargo craft could take Button's consignments down to Bristol, to be trans-shipped into an ocean-going vessel.

We know the names of some of the ships associated with Button Gwinnett's transatlantic ventures during the years 1761 and 1762: *Polly, Garland, New Grace, Nancy* and *Bristol Packet* sailed to Boston, Philadelphia and New York. Button's share varied considerably, from a small part of the cargo to the whole. On one voyage, for example, he had a twenty-five per cent interest in the cargo of the *Nancy* and, at a later date, was sole owner of the ship. The vessels seem amazingly small: the *Bristol Packet* entered Boston harbour on 26 October 1762 and was recorded as being a brig of ninety tons, manned by a crew of seven.

Anyone looking to make money in this trade had to be successful not only in obtaining credit, but also competent at managing the cash flow. This was Button Gwinnett's weakness. Like almost all the traders, Button bought goods on credit and exported them, but he had a poor record when it came to payment of his debts. The Georgia State Archive in Atlanta has documents revealing the names of people who tried to get money out of him, including Bentley and Boardman (Liverpool), Sheppard, Langton and Bailey (Liverpool), Durand and Phillips (Canada), Thomas and Ferdinand Pennington (Bristol).

GWINNETT

The Penningtons called in the bailiffs, who impounded the *Nancy* at Bristol, and sold her to pay off Button's debts.

At intervals during his commercial operations Button went home to Wolverhampton, where he is listed (1761) as a subscriber to the Blue Coat charity school. He also found time to visit his brother at Cottrell, which was an easy trip, given the frequent sailings of passenger-carrying boats between Bristol and Cardiff or Aberthaw. Samuel Gwinnett made a note of "My brother's visit of affection from Canada in the spring of 1761."

Four years after this visit, Button decided to move the base of his business to the New World. He opened a shop in Savannah, advertising in the *Georgia Gazette* of 26 September 1765:

Just imported

To be sold on the most reasonable terms, by

BUTTON GWINNETT

At the store lately occupied by Messrs. Johnson and Wylly,

The following goods, viz.

RHUBARB - Turlington's balsam of life, - Dr. James's powders for fevers, - flake manna, - glauber salts, - Florence oil, - mustard, - tin ware, - ironmongery, - plain, silver, and gold laced hats, - breeches pieces, - silk and thread hose, - jewelery, - pickles, - cutlery, - saddlery, - earthen and delft ware, - mould candles, - fine beer, - glass, - shoes, - sheeting, - canvas, - oznaburgs, - Irish linens, - cheques, - paint, - cheese, - butter, - nails, - cyder, - Scots barley, - English manufactured tobacco, - vinegar, - bed furniture, and many other articles too tedious to insert.

The British possessions in America were strung out over fifteen hundred miles of the Atlantic coast and each colony was independent of the others, with its own governor, assembly and currency. One factor in his decision to emigrate may well have been the end of the Seven Years War in 1763: the French and Spanish territories of north America were transferred to the British crown (in the person of the twenty-five year old George III) and the acquisition of Florida meant that Georgia would at last be free from threats of Spanish incursions. In addition the local Indians were, for the moment, quiescent.

Button Gwinnett's new home of Georgia was poor and sparsely populated. Savannah, where Button's store was to be found, was the chief town and social centre of Georgia. There were plenty of places to get a drink (ten licensed, and twelve not), a subscription library and a newspaper founded two years before. Seekers after entertainment could attend horse races, cricket matches, and occasional theatrical performances. On special occasions dinners and balls were arranged:

for the King's birthday, St. George's day, St. Patrick's day and Guy Fawkes night.

The other main settlement developed at Sunbury, which was declared an official "port of entry" in 1762. From the town three islands could be seen, away in the distance, across the creeks and marshes. One of these islands would soon be Button Gwinnett's. Georgia has a coastal plain about ten miles wide, broken up by a tortuous maze of estuaries and salt marshes. The whole coastline has a chain of "barrier" islands, separated from the mainland by sea and marsh. The islands are low-lying, hot, humid and (in the eighteenth century) unhealthy. Button Gwinnett now bought one - on credit, of course. His restless journeying had brought him from St. Catharine's (Gloucester) to St. Catharine's (Georgia).

St. Catharine's Island, about ten miles away from Sunbury, had been surveyed in 1760 and found to be 6250 acres in extent. The survey map shows it hemmed in on the landward side by several "large marshes". Button Gwinnett sold his store in Savannah and took out a lease of the island for five hundred years. For the island, buildings, cattle, timber and boat he paid £3,000, all of it borrowed. Acquiring the property brought about an instant improvement in Button's social status: instead of being "Button Gwinnett, Merchant", he was now "Button Gwinnett, of St. Catharine's Island, Esquire". His land-holding qualified him as an elector, and led to his appointment as a Justice of the Peace (1767) and as Commissioner for regulating estuary pilotage (1768).

As well as becoming a landowner, Button was now a slave-owner. He started off with fourteen slaves - bought on credit - some of whom had come straight from their homes in Africa. A direct trade in slaves had just begun to Florida, as reported in the *Massachusetts Gazette* on Christmas Eve 1767. The brigantine *Augustine* had just carried to St. Augustine "seventy negroes from Africa, the first ever imported directly from thence into that province... Upwards of 2000 were contracted for by the noblemen and gentlemen of Great Britain... to be imported there from Africa the ensuing summer".

Button Gwinnett was doing well, and his letters to his brother at Cottrell must have been full of optimism: he was a landowner (more acres than Cottrell!), had agricultural and business interests, was a Justice, River Pilotage Commissioner and now (1769) he was elected to Georgia's Commons House of Assembly (a compact body of fewer than thirty members). Button attended only one session and then pulled out. Sinking under an increasing weight of debt, he took out a second mortgage on the island and mortgaged six of his slaves: Cleo, Cuff, Doll, Sam, Qua and Quamina. A few months later he sold Boston,

GWINNETT

Advertisements from the Georgia Gazette 1765 and 1766.

> **Just imported,**
> To be sold on the most reasonable terms, by
> **BUTTON GWINNETT,**
> At the store lately occupied by Messrs. Johnson and Wylly,
> **THE FOLLOWING GOODS, viz.**
>
> RHUBARB,—Turlington's balsam of life,—Dr. James's powders for fevers,—flake manna,—glauber salts,—Florence oil,—mustard,—tin ware,—ironmongery,—plain, silver, and gold laced hats,—breeches pieces,—silk and thread hose,—jewelery,—pickles,—cutlery,—saddlery,—earthen and delft ware,—mould candles,—fine beer,—glass,—shoes,—sheeting,—canvass,—oznaburgs,—Irish linens,—cheques,—paint,—cheese,—butter,—nails,—cyder,—Scots barley,—English manufactured tobacco,—vinegar,—bed furniture,—and many other articles too tedious to insert.

> **To be Leased for a Number of Years,**
> THE VALUABLE ISLAND of ST. CATHERINE, with the STOCK and CATTLE, and the USE of the TIMBER.—For particulars enquire of the Rev. Mr. Bosomworth on the said island, or of GREY ELLIOTT.

> ALL persons whatever are hereby prohibited from hunting and shooting upon the Island of Saint Catherine's, or causelessly landing upon the same, or fishing on the shore or beach, or in any of the creeks thereunto belonging, as such trespassers, when known, will be prosecuted without distinction to the utmost rigour of the law. AND WHEREAS loose and disorderly people have frequently killed and carried off from the said island hogs and cattle, to the great loss of the subscriber, to prevent such practices for the future, I do hereby offer a reward of twenty pounds sterling to any person or persons who shall discover any person who has been or may hereafter be guilty thereof, to be paid upon conviction of the offender; and if any person, who may have been concerned, or hereafter may be concerned, in such practices, will discover and give evidence against his accomplice or accomplices, such person shall be entitled to and receive the same reward from   BUTTON GWINNETT

Cicero, Damie, Doll and her children (Flora and Judith), Jacob, Mary and Monday. Matters came to a head early in 1773 when his creditors called a meeting, at which they insisted on the sale of St. Catharine's Island, the animals, the timber and the boat. Button persuaded them to let him continue living on the island.

The Political Button

A crisis had been reached in Button Gwinnett's financial affairs. There was also a more general, political, financial crisis - one which was to result in the destruction of all links between Crown and Colonies.

Fighting Indians and the French had led to increased taxation in

Britain, not to mention a doubling of the national debt. The British government felt that it was time that the American colonies paid something towards their own defence, but the colonials would have none of it. Parliament brought in measures to raise money - from the colonists for the defence of the colonists - and all hell broke loose. The home government introduced the Coercive Acts, which stirred up more resistance. A writer to the *Georgia Gazette,* rehearsing the colonists' grievances, came to the conclusion that: "If we are no longer allowed the rights of Britons, **we must** be Americans".

Back in London, Lord North and his government believed that they could pick off the colonies one by one. They thought, as did many in America, that the colonies would be unable to work together to achieve their aims. This prognostication was wrong, and the various colonies, to co-ordinate their actions, met at a Continental Congress in Philadelphia (September 1774). No one from Georgia turned up, and the delegates decided that they could only "lament Georgia with resentment".

Fighting broke out in many places, and soon the Royal Governor of Georgia was asking for more money, soldiers and ships to help keep order. By July he felt that Georgia was lost to the crown. (The colonists were not all of one mind: John Adams reckoned that a third took up arms, a third supported King George, and a third did not give a damn either way. Another "distempered and bedlam time" had begun.)

Button Gwinnett, meanwhile, was again becoming active in public affairs. He was to be seen lobbying his fellow Whigs in Georgia's rural parishes and those on his side came to be known as the **Country** or **Popular Party** whose aim was to wrest power from the **City** or **Conservative Party.** In January 1776 Button Gwinnett was chosen as one of the Georgia delegates to the Second Continental Congress. Arriving in Philadelphia in May, after a journey of seven hundred miles, Button joined in: he served on several committees, voted for and signed the Declaration of Independence which renounced allegiance to Crown and Parliament. A month later the Declaration was read aloud publicly in Savannah, with much feasting and the drinking of toasts to the "United, Free and Independent States of America".

Back home, Button became involved in various meetings to set up a new apparatus of government for Georgia. He was elected Speaker of the legislature and chaired the committee drawing up a new constitution for the State. In the middle of February 1777 most of the members of the Provincial Congress went home, leaving responsibility for the day-to-day business of government in the hands of a Council of Safety under the President, Alexander Bulloch. He died a fortnight later, whereupon the Council of Safety elected Button Gwinnett to be

GWINNETT

President in his place.

The first Assembly under the new constitution met in May 1777 when Button Gwinnett was disappointed not to be elected as Governor. During the debate Lachlan McIntosh called Button "a scoundrel and a lying rascal". Relations between the two men had long been deteriorating - they had been rivals for the command of the militia, Button had gaoled Lachlan's brother, and there had been friction over Button's ill-judged military expedition against East Florida (from whence the "Florida Scouts", loyal to the crown, had been foraging into Georgia). Button Gwinnett challenged Lachlan McIntosh to a duel, with pistols, in which both men were wounded. McIntosh recovered, but Button Gwinnett (aged forty-two) died three days later on 19 May 1777. It is ironic that Button Gwinnett - whose brother lived at Cottrell for forty years - should be done to death by a member of the Clan Mackintosh. A century later that clan's Chief would live at Cottrell for almost sixty years.

Emilia Gwinnett

The death of Button Gwinnett in 1777 meant that only two of his brothers and sisters were still alive: Samuel (the owner of Cottrell) and Emilia.

Emilia was nine years younger than her Reverend brother, and she may well have spent some years looking after her Reverend father at Down Hatherley. When he died, she was thirty-four and began to

Emilia Gwinnett.

Penlline Castle, as it was when inherited by Emilia Gwinnett from her friend Lady Vernon. As well as the picturesque ruin Emilia obtained a house and the income from the estate.

spend more time at Cottrell, becoming a close friend of Lady Vernon who owned Penlline Castle, a quick trip down the new turnpike road which passed Cottrell's gates.

Louisa Barbara Vernon was born in 1733, daughter and heir of Bussy Mansel, 4th Baron Mansel of Margam (Louisa's mother was a daughter of William Villiers, 2nd Earl of Jersey - this Villiers connection has a bearing on the later ownership of Cottrell). Louisa Mansel was married at the age of twenty-four, at St. George's Hanover Square, to the twenty-two year old George Venables Vernon. The future Lord Vernon and Baron Kinderton had been educated at Westminster School and Trinity Hall, Cambridge. (The family seat, Sudbury Hall near Derby, is today in the care of the National Trust.) His wife brought her own estates to the marriage including Newick Place (a delightful house in Sussex), the Briton Ferry estate, and Penlline Castle. George and Louisa produced two daughters - after eight years of marriage Louisa Barbarina was born, followed three years later by Charlotte who died before reaching her second birthday. Married for almost thirty years, the union seems to have been an unhappy one, and the couple became estranged and lived apart. Louisa was denied access to her daughter, who died at the age of nineteen, to be followed eight months later by her mother. After a further three months the widower married again.

Louisa had died, aged fifty-three, at her house in Portman Square, London, where one of her Villiers relations (later to become Earl of Clarendon) found a sealed envelope in a drawer. It contained Louisa's will. This was an unusual one, in that Louisa Vernon had made alterations, without witnesses, in her own handwriting - crossing out the names of some of the original beneficiaries and substituting new ones, including Emilia Gwinnett. Lady Vernon left Penlline Castle to:

> *Emilia Gwinnett, spinster, of Cottrell in Glamorganshire...*
> *for her friendly attention to me in all my troubles, with this*
> *request: that she would add to the Castle and reside there*
> *mostly in summer.*

The amended will disinherited close family members and at the end of the document Lady Vernon wrote a note explaining why she had done this:

> *The reason of my taking but little notice of my near relations*
> *is because they have never thought fit to assist me in my*
> *troubles or ever made a point of my getting my child, but*
> **Vernon** *is the sole cause of my child being disinherited for*
> *which she has reason to thank him. And the reason for my*
> *parting with him which I now make known to the world was*
> *his attachment and intimacy with Ann Brown his daughter's*
> *maid, which many can testify to the truth of... and other*
> *intimacies well known... I hope he will be forgiven in the*
> *next world.*

She added:

> *I desire all my dogs may be carried to Miss Emily Gwinnett,*
> *wherever she is and I request that the Box I always keep under*
> *my bed be opened and examined by Miss Gwinnett - about the*
> *contents she knows what to do with* (26 August 1783)

As a consequence of Lord Vernon's infidelities, Emilia Gwinnett became, unexpectedly, a wealthy landowner in her own right. A castle had stood at Penlline for over seven hundred years, on a bluff overlooking the River Thaw. The estate descended through various Turbervilles and Stradlings to the Mansel family and to Louisa Mansel (Lady Vernon). In 1652 the castle was described as ruined, but adjoining it, or in place of it, "a fair house". For Emilia Gwinnett it was, of course, not simply a question of inheriting a house and a picturesque ruin. With them came all the income from the estate, so it was not difficult for her to comply with Lady Vernon's request that she should "add to the castle", which she did between 1789 and 1804.

Cottrell

Six years after inheriting Penlline, Emilia Gwinnett was to have the Cottrell estate as well, on the death of her brother Samuel. To place this in context, here is a reminder of the owners of Cottrell during the eighteenth century:

		Inherited
	Barbara Button	1718
Barbara's cousin:	Emilia Button	1755
Emilia's husband:	Samuel Gwinnett	1755
Samuel's sister:	Emilia Gwinnett	1792

There is a tradition that Emilia Gwinnett obtained the Cottrell estate by skulduggery - by burning her brother's will immediately after his death. The mansion of Cottrell is no more but while it stood Emilia, full of remorse, haunted parts of it - or so they say!

Now owning both Penlline and Cottrell, Miss Emilia Gwinnett shot up the league table of landowners in the Vale. Her two estates made her seventh in the order, just below the Earl of Plymouth and the Marquess of Bute. As with most people who possessed large estates, Emilia employed an agent to undertake the management and was fortunate to secure the services of John Franklen, a leading agriculturalist and a prime mover in the founding of the Glamorgan Agricultural Society. He also instituted an annual March market in Cowbridge which became known as "Franklen's Fair". In the 1750s he had become agent to Lady Charlotte Edwin at Llanmihangel, where the farm became almost a "demonstration" one. Such a man must have kept Cottrell in good order. (In 1799 Emilia Gwinnett was awarded a medal for "best bull" by the county Agricultural Society.)

Emilia Gwinnett makes a brief appearance in the diaries of John Bird, clerk to the first Marquess of Bute. An entry for 2 May 1792, a few months after Samuel Gwinnett's demise concerns payment of a *heriot*: a fine paid to the landlord on the death of a tenant. It was usually "the best beast", although a cash payment might be accepted instead. On her brother's death, Emilia had paid the *heriot* for some property at Miskin, but John Bird discovered that another was due, this time for land rented by Samuel Gwinnett at Eglwysylan (not far from Senghennydd).

John Bird visited Miss Gwinnett at Cottrell, where she told him that she would instruct Mr. Franklen to make the payment. Emilia then asked John Bird if the Marquess of Bute, his employer, had left Bath yet. She wanted to ask Lord Bute a favour: to arrange for her friend, David Samuel (Bonvilston) to be made a Justice of the Peace. He had an income of £500 a year and was willing to act both as Justice and Deputy-Lieutenant. Her late brother had filled the latter office, and she hoped her friend could do the same.

In August of the following year, Emilia was involved in a legal action. The case, heard in Cardiff before Judge Hardinge, was an action of trespass brought by a Penlline farmer. It was alleged that, almost a year before, her gamekeeper had gone into two fields of barley "and wantonly beaten about for game therein". Defence counsel argued that the action was brought maliciously but, after a trial lasting five hours, the court found that three bushels of barley had been spoiled and awarded the plaintiff thirty shillings damages and his costs. John Bird wrote to Lord Bute that "this will cost Miss Gwinnett from fifty to sixty pounds".

We may deduce something of life at Cottrell at this time by reading the diary kept by John Perkins of Llantrithyd. He was a gentleman farmer, by no means as wealthy as Emilia Gwinnett, but as neighbours they had the same local background to their daily lives.

John Perkins did not travel much but, like Emilia, had relatives who did. (His brother was in India, and other relations were in Jamaica and Madeira.) His own journeys were more local: to Aberthaw to buy

Emilia Gwinnett's bookplate.

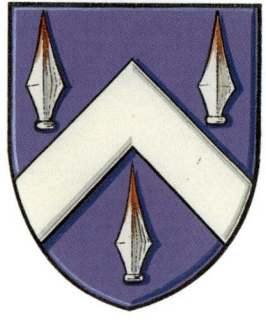

Arms of the Gwinnett family, owners of Cottrell from 1755 to 1807.

Arms of the Tyler family.

Arms of The Mackintosh.

imported goods and to Cowbridge on Tuesdays for the market. Like most of his neighbours he enjoyed attending race meetings. He mentions a number of itinerants who would also have been regular callers at Cottrell, including a candle seller, hawkers, tinkers and Tom the Collier. The diary helps us to imagine the kinds of people employed, on and off, at Cottrell: "serving women", women to brew beer, tailors, watch and clock repairers and chimney sweeps. There were glaziers, masons, sawyers and thatchers, as well as general labourers.

John Perkins subscribed to Bristol and London journals and was a regular borrower from the Cowbridge and Llancarfan Book Society. We know that he read *Tristram Shandy*, which was first published in instalments from 1760 to 1767. If Emilia Gwinnett also read it, she would have paused as she came to the words "There is a north-west passage of the intellect". Her thoughts would have turned towards Sir Thomas Button, dead for a hundred and fifty years, but whose ghost still galloped around St. Nicholas. His silver-topped cane was a treasured possession of Emilia's.

As well as the civilized pursuit of reading, Emilia Gwinnett may have involved herself in another agreeable task, that of re-arranging the landscape for pleasure. In the late eighteenth and early nineteenth centuries, the formal garden went out of fashion in favour of the more casual look - planning to make the landscape appear unplanned. The idea was that the acres around your house should appear to be natural, by featuring rolling grassland, carefully placed trees, and streams, lakes and bridges. These could be best appreciated from artfully placed "viewing platforms". A number of these features were introduced at Cottrell, including an avenue of trees laid out eastwards from the motte, as far as the lane. It may be that this was intended as a new, grander entrance to the grounds, sweeping across grassland, taking a close look at the motte, before a gradual bend leading towards the woods. Tantalising glimpses of the house would have been contrived. The motte itself may have been used as a ready-made viewing platform; it has mature trees on top today, and these may have been planted to impress, as well as to provide shade or shelter. It is likely that the cottage at the park gates was re-modelled at this time.

Writing in the year of Emilia's death (1807), the traveller B.H. Malkin observed that "the village of St. Nicholas has nothing very remarkable about it except some very neat cottages with uncommonly pretty gardens". He saw, near the Cottrell gates, an ancient and well-known beech tree. "At the height of six feet it girts twenty feet. At the height of about sixteen or eighteen feet it divides into two large limbs. - It is a grand object, and has not the least appearance of decay". A hundred and thirty years later, Charles Shepherd noted that the tree

GWINNETT

Chatham Dockyard, where Charles Tyler joined his first ship (HMS Barfleur) in 1771. He was eleven years old.

was still there, with its trunk strengthened by iron bands.

Emilia Gwinnett's will runs to twenty-seven densely written pages. The executor, and also a beneficiary, was Thomas, Earl of Clarendon - the same man who acted as executor of Lady Vernon's will twenty-one years earlier. Penlline Castle was to be given to Emilia's relative, William Chute Hayton of Wistaston Court, on condition that he changed his name to Gwinnett. There were other conditions:

> *I direct that all my furniture, my plate, my musical instruments, china, books, towels, trinkets, precious stones, shells and fossils to remain and continue at my mansion house of Penlline to be kept and used.*

But "my silver-headed cane said to be taken by Admiral Sir Thomas Button in the Spanish Armada" was bequeathed to Thomas Mansel Talbot. The new occupants of Penlline were to take care of "my little horse called Squirrel" for the rest of his life, and he was not to do "any manner of work whatsoever".

Emilia made extraordinary arrangements for her dogs and birds. They were to be cared for by Emilia's housekeeper, Jane Lewis. If Jane were to die, then Frances Dawkins was to take over. Dogs, birds and minders were very well provided for: £20 a quarter to feed the dogs and birds, plus an allowance for the humans. The pets were to live with their keeper in a cottage which was provided. The new owners of Penlline "shall give full and free permission for all and any of the said dogs to run over or about the lands or grounds... without any hindrance or molestation".

Emilia Gwinnett asked "to be buried at Newick in the County of Sussex as near the remains of the late Lady Louisa Barbara Vernon as may be". She was so buried on 30 September 1807.

The burned will: a denouement?

The allegation was that Emilia obtained Cottrell by burning her brother's will. What was in that will, which so offended Emilia, and tempted her to such a drastic act? Her own will provides clues to a possible explanation.

Emilia Gwinnett bequeathed Cottrell to the Earl of Clarendon for his life, but thereafter:

> *I do hereby give and devise the same (Cottrell) unto George Tyler eldest son of Charles Tyler ... by Margaret his wife (late Margaret Leach) and to the heirs and assigns of the said George Tyler the son for ever.*

What prompted Emilia to do this? Why should Charles and Margaret Tyler's son George receive such a munificent gift? The reason, as passed down in the Tyler family, was:

Samuel Gwinnett wished to marry Margaret Leach, but she married Charles Tyler instead.

Samuel, still fond of Margaret, left Cottrell to her in his will. Samuel's sister Emilia resented this, and destroyed the will.

In her own will, she tried to put matters right by leaving Cottrell to Margaret's son. This sounds like a plausible explanation, and the dates could fit:

October 1785	Samuel Gwinnett's wife dies.
1786/1787	Samuel becomes a suitor for the hand of Miss Leach. He is 53, she is 26.
November 1788	Miss Leach marries Charles Tyler.
January 1792	Samuel Gwinnett dies. His will is destroyed.

Emilia Gwinnett's will (drawn up during her final illness) may be seen as an act of atonement for having deprived Margaret Leach and her heirs of their inheritance. Emilia settled the Cottrell estates where, in due course, they should have gone - to the eldest son of Margaret Leach (now Tyler). George Tyler was only fourteen at this time, so it made sense to have an "interim" beneficiary: the Earl of Clarendon, who was fifty-three, and unmarried.

5. Clarendon

The second Earl of Clarendon became involved with Cottrell because he was a Villiers relative of Lady Vernon. Through her he became acquainted with Emilia Gwinnett, and agreed to act as her executor. It is probable that he came to regret this, as the will became the subject of an action in the High Court of Chancery: The Reverend John Morgan sued the Earl for payment of Emilia's debt of £1,700 incurred in 1799. Richard Griffiths was owed money for "medical advice and assistance, medicines, attendances, and services", and there were several other claimants on the estate.

Involvement with the Court of Chancery was to be avoided, if at all possible, because of its long-winded and costly proceedings, and uncertain outcome. Charles Dickens in *Bleak House* described the results of actions in the Court of Chancery:

> ... which has its decaying houses and its blighted lands in every shire; which has its worn out lunatic in every madhouse, and its dead in every churchyard; which has its ruined suitor, with his slipshod heels and threadbare dress, borrowing and begging through the round of every man's acquaintance; which gives to monied might the means abundantly of

BELOW:
HMS Hydra. Charles Tyler (the younger) deserted from this ship at Malta because (according to Nelson) of "an unfortunate desire to travel ... and perhaps an imprudent attachment to an Italian lady".

wearying out the right; which so exhausts finances, patience, courage, hope; so overthrows the brain and breaks the heart; that there is not an honourable man among its practitioners who would not give - who does not often give - the warning 'suffer any wrong that can be done to you, rather than come here!'.

The judgement concerning Emilia Gwinnett's will took nearly nine years to emerge. The Court ordered that some of Emilia's personal effects be sold to clear part of the debt, which led to an auction by Mr. Sotheby in October 1816 of **Books, Prints and Manuscripts, part of the personal estate of Miss Emilia Gwinnett.** The sale raised more than £460, from 691 lots, over three days. Included were many books belonging to her father and brother (the two Samuel Gwinnetts) - theology, philosophy, Latin and Greek tomes as well as novels and plays. The younger Samuel's early manuscripts were there, including his play *The Appian Violence* and two morocco-bound copies of *Lusus Pueriles*. The spirit of Rice Merrick was conjured up by *A Volume containing the Pedigrees of the Principal Welch Families, beginning with Adam.*

The Earl of Clarendon never lived at Cottrell and the estate entered a kind of limbo, which continued until the Chancery action was concluded. For a while, James Phelp rented the house. There is a will (of March 1812, with a codicil of June 1814) "of me James Phelp late

CLARENDON

Thomas Villiers, second Earl of Clarendon, who inherited Cottrell from Emilia Gwinnett.
He was immediately involved in a Chancery dispute over the will.

of Coston in the County of Leicester but now of Cottrell House in the County of Glamorgan, Esquire". James Phelp's daughter, and his son, both married into the Powell family of Nanteos. James Phelp was part of a syndicate formed to build Assembly Rooms in Aberystwyth, on land owned by the young William Edward Powell who married Laura Phelp (thus: Laura Gardens and Laura Place in Aberystwyth).

William Powell was more interested in Bath and Newmarket than in a Welsh seaside resort, and his mother was also piling up debts, fleeing to Boulogne to escape her creditors. It was, surely, time for her daughter to marry a wealthy man. Instead, Ellen chose James Phelp's son: Edward Tufton Phelp. Two Phelps in the family was too much for the elder Mrs. Powell, who described her intended son-in-law as "a gentleman of large family and small fortune". (Although his father, in his will, reckoned that his son was "amply provided for".) Mrs. Powell wrote angrily to her son (in 1811): "Is it true that he **plays** and belongs to several public hunts and clubs, which even in a man of fortune would be an insurmountable objection."

COTTRELL

Cottrell House in the 1820s, from a contemporary watercolour by Charlotte Traherne.

After James Phelp it looks as if the house was occupied by William and Anne Maynard. The St. Nicholas church register has an entry for 27 July 1813 recording the baptism of "Walter, son of William and Anne Maynard, of Cottrell House" and there are two advertisements in the *Cambrian News* (8 January and 5 February 1814) for an auction of household furniture, hay and a horse and cart "at Cottrell House, occupied by W. Maynard". Two months later the same newspaper was advertising "Cottrell House to let, lately held by Colonel Phelp. Apply John Franklen, Cowbridge".

The Chancery case at last came to an end, Mr. Sotheby held his sale, and any claims on the estate were finally settled. The legal position was now:

> The Earl of Clarendon held Cottrell for the rest of his life.
>
> On the Earl's death, the estate was to pass to George Tyler (eldest son of Charles and Margaret Tyler).

CLARENDON

What happened was:

> **Charles** Tyler occupied Cottrell and Gwreiddin as the Earl's tenant.
>
> When the Earl died, the estate became **George** Tyler's, but his father continued to live there.

Charles Tyler came to Cottrell in 1817 and in April 1824 is still listed (in the Poor Relief Rate Book) as a tenant. The Earl of Clarendon died in 1824 (as did his agent, John Franklen) and George Tyler came into his inheritance. His father, Admiral Sir Charles Tyler lived on the estate for the rest of his life, occupying Cottrell House from 1817 to 1835, a period of eighteen years.

THE BREACH

"The Breach" consisted of two estate cottages. They are still there, on the right of the main road (going towards Cowbridge), halfway between the Lodge and the crossroads.

Some of the people who lived there in the Earl of Clarendon's time were:

1813	William and Hannah Owen Son: James	Blacksmith
1815	William and Mary Jenkins Children: John (died aged one year), Mary, John	Labourer
	Philip and Elizabeth Griffiths Son: Philip	Labourer
1816	Catherine Lewis (died, aged 26)	
	Thomas and Anne Richards Sons: Thomas and William	Cooper

The fall of Nelson. Although this painting shows HMS Victory the scene on Tonnant must have been similar. Like Admiral Nelson, Captain Tyler was hit by a musket ball and had to be taken below, leaving Lieutenant John Bedford in command.

Trafalgar - the beginning of the action. Captain Tyler's ship Tonnant was the fourth ship in the lee column. As she moved slowly towards the enemy the ship's band played "Britons strike home!"

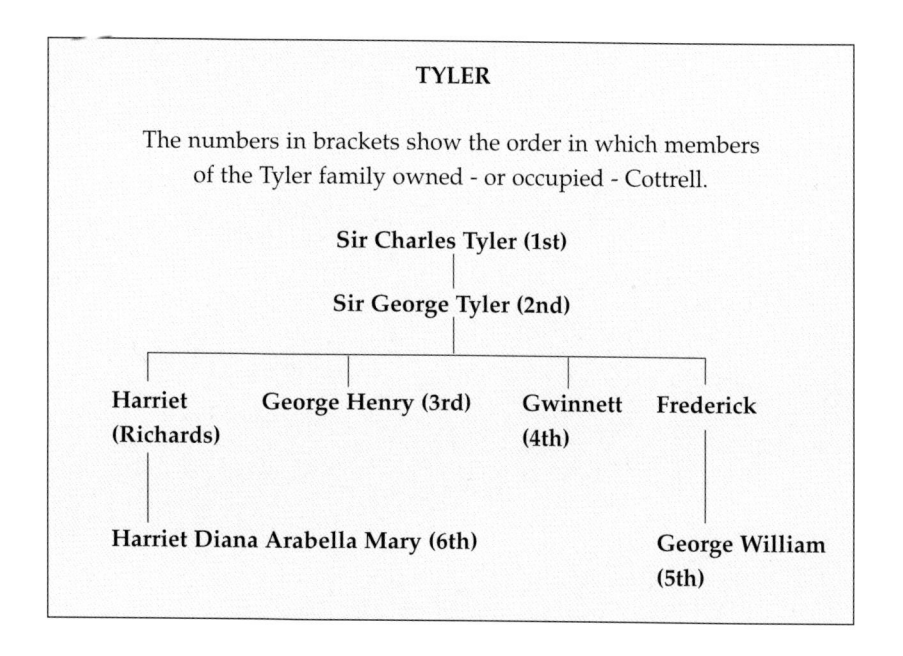

```
                                TYLER

      The numbers in brackets show the order in which members
            of the Tyler family owned - or occupied - Cottrell.

                        Sir Charles Tyler (1st)
                                 |
                        Sir George Tyler (2nd)
          ┌──────────────┬──────────────┬──────────────┐
       Harriet      George Henry (3rd)  Gwinnett    Frederick
      (Richards)                         (4th)         |
          |                                            |
   Harriet Diana Arabella Mary (6th)            George William
                                                    (5th)
```

6. Tyler

Sir Charles Tyler

Admiral Sir Charles Tyler had just left active service when he arrived to take up residence at Cottrell. Of his fifty-seven years, forty-six had been spent in the Royal Navy, in a career which reached its apogee when he captained a warship at the Battle of Trafalgar, serving under the command of his friend, Horatio Nelson.

It is not possible, here, to describe such a varied, active and lengthy career in any detail. The aim will be to give a general impression, and take note of the highlights.

Charles's father was Peter Tyler, Irishman, and an officer in the 52nd Regiment (Oxfordshire Light Infantry) who married Anne Roper, daughter of the eighth Lord Teynham. Charles was one of five children and spent most of his early years in Ireland where his father's regiment was stationed; later in life he was described as speaking with a slight "Irish brogue".

North America

In 1771 Charles joined his first ship the *Barfleur* (90) - the figure in brackets shows the number of guns carried by the vessel, and is an

Sir Charles Tyler's Ships

(The number in brackets shows the number of guns.)

April 1771	*Barfleur* (90)	Chatham
September 1771	*Arethusa* (38)	North America
1774-1778	*Preston* (50)	North America
1779	*Culloden* (74)	Channel Fleet
1780-1782	*Britannia* (100)	Channel Fleet
1782	*Edgar*	Channel Fleet
1783	*Queen* (20) *Chapman*	South Shields South Shields
1784-1789	*Trimmer*	Milford Haven
1790	*Tisiphone*	Channel Fleet

As a Post-Captain, he commanded:

1790	*Maidstone* (28)	Channel Fleet
1793-1794	*Meleager* (32)	Mediterranean
1794-1796	*Diadem* (64)	Mediterranean
1796-1798	*L'Aigle* (38)	Mediterranean
1798-1802	*Warrior* (74)	Atlantic, Baltic, W. Indies
1805	*Tonnant* (80)	Trafalgar

indication of its size. (A 1st Rate had 100 guns - a 5th Rate had 30 to 40, and a 6th Rate, 20 or 30 guns.) *HMS Barfleur* was a 2nd Rate, with a complement of 750 men, and had been launched only three years earlier. When Charles Tyler joined, she was guardship at Chatham dockyard.

The eleven year old boy was taken on as "servant" to Captain Andrew Snape Hamond. This was the usual way for prospective naval officers to enter at this time, starting a career as a personal "follower" of the captain, usually to oblige relatives. (Nelson began in this way, in the same year as Charles Tyler). It was not an easy life; not long before, Samuel Johnson had written: "No man will be a sailor who has contrivance enough to get himself into jail; for being in a ship is being in a jail, with the chance of being drowned... A man in jail has more room, better food, and commonly better company". The social position of the naval officer was, however, slowly improving and many families now steered their sons towards the sea. Jane Austen's two brothers, for example, made successful careers in the Royal Navy.

After five months at Chatham, Charles transferred, with Captain Hamond, to *HMS Arethusa* (38), a captured French frigate. They sailed immediately for the navy's North American station. After two-and-a-half years in the *Arethusa*, Charles was moved to *Preston* (50) the flagship of Admiral Samuel Graves. The "Boston Tea Party" had taken place in December 1773 and the British government decided that

Admiral Sir Charles Tyler (1760-1835).

OPPOSITE:
A map of the Cottrell estate, from the sale particulars of 1942. The numbers refer to the "Summary of Lots" (see page 117).

BELOW:
Fort Charlotte, St. Vincent. George Tyler was lieutenant-governor of the island from 1833-1840.

"effectual steps be taken to secure the dependence of the colonies on the mother country". Admiral Graves was ordered to close the port of Boston, which he did with the aid of *Preston, Royal Oak, Egmont* and *Worcester.*

Midshipman Tyler was on board *Preston*, and there is a family belief that both he and his father were at the Battle of Bunker Hill in June 1775 - Peter Tyler with the 52nd Regiment and Charles on one of the bombarding vessels. The *Preston* was certainly engaged in several major actions (often involving the transport and landing of troops), including operations in 1776 around New York, New Jersey and the Hudson river. For example, on 22nd August 1776 a large British force was put ashore on Long Island with the aim of taking the high ground as a prelude to an attack on New York. Nine thousand men - half of Washington's army - defended the heights. By noon on the 22nd, the British had landed 15,000 soldiers and forty field guns; by the 27th, the force totalled 25,000, all of whom had been transported and protected by the Royal Navy (the boat landings being under the command of William Hotham, in *HMS Preston*.) Faced with overwhelming odds, the Americans withdrew silently, by night, with all their arms and equipment. This highly-disciplined manoeuvre saved half of Washington's command.

The final naval act of the campaign of August-December 1776 was the British occupation of Rhode Island. On 8th December, the *Preston*, with four other ships-of-the-line and eight smaller vessels,

TYLER

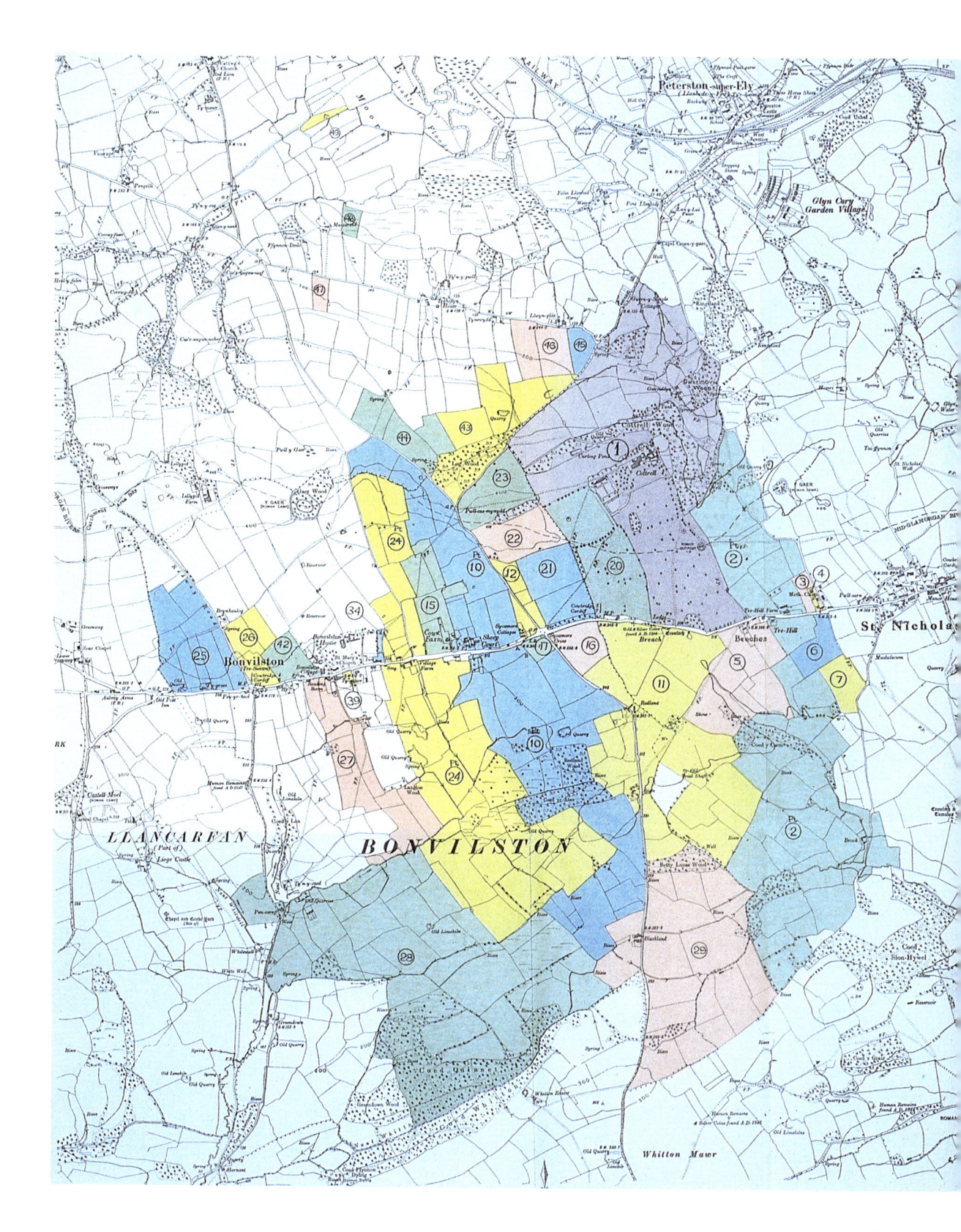

landed seven thousand men at Newport, thus closing a privateering haven and securing a good base for naval operations. *Preston* was also part of Howe's fleet manoeuvering for battle with the French fleet (under de Guichen) on 11th August 1778 when a ferocious storm blew up, scattering the protagonists and causing a good deal of damage.

During his service off the American coast, Charles sustained a leg injury, caused by frostbite. Years later he petitioned George III:

> *While on duty in America in the year 1777 by the extreme severity of the weather, your petitioner was so injured in his left leg as to render it necessary to remove a small bone in consequence of which he was upwards of two years unable to move except upon crutches.*

He walked with a limp for ever after.

European Waters

The next ship to embark Charles Tyler was *Culloden* (74), part of the Channel Fleet. During his time on board, he was promoted to the rank of lieutenant, the promotion board being satisfied that "he can splice, knot, reef a sail, etc. and is qualified to do the duty of an able Seaman and Midshipman". As a lieutenant he went to *Britannia* (100), taking part in attacks on convoys and being part of a flotilla which relieved the garrison of Gibraltar. On 10th December 1781 a French convoy left Brest escorted by a force commanded by de Guichen. A British fleet (under Richard Kempenfelt), which had left England eight days earlier, was waiting to intercept. Admiral Kempenfelt's ships included *Victory* and *Britannia* (with Lieutenant Charles Tyler). The French escorts found themselves ahead and to leeward of their charges, and were unable to intervene as the British approached. The convoy scattered, but Kempenfelt's force captured fifteen ships, leaving only two sail-of-the-line and five transports to continue to the Caribbean.

Lieutenant Tyler was now put to work in smaller vessels: *Queen* (20), *Chapman*, and *Trimmer*. These were his first independent commands, stationed first at South Shields and later at Milford Haven. Joining *Queen* in January 1783, he was to spend more than seven years employed on similar duties. *Trimmer* was a sloop, based at Milford Haven. Charles Tyler's orders were to patrol the Bristol Channel and further afield, roughly within the sea area Cardiff-Milford Haven-Land's End. To do this he was allocated *Trimmer*, *Viper* and *Spider* - it was, almost, Sir Thomas Button's old command.

There were occasional diversions. On 30 September 1787 he was on board *Trimmer*, near the mouth of the Bristol Avon, in charge of a press-gang:

> *I immediately began pressing all the men I found on board ships ready for sea to the number of thirty.*

TYLER

Altogether he managed to collar eighty-five men, keeping twenty for his own vessels and sending the rest to Portsmouth.

CHARLES TYLER (the younger)

An outline of the career of Charles Tyler's son by his first marriage.

Born: 15 April 1784

Entered Royal Navy 1796

1796   *L'Aigle* (38)   Midshipman. His father was captain.

In the Mediterranean he served on:

Marlborough (74)

Warrior (74)   His father was captain.

Champion (24)

Lion (64)

1800   *Warrior*, his father's ship, in the Baltic.

1801   *Alcimene*   Promoted to lieutenant.

Then to (1805)   *Hydra* (38)

Elephant (74)

Iris (36)

December 1809   *Arrogant*

April 1811   *Hesper* (18)

November 1811   *Procris* (18)   Java.

December 1811 (aged 27)   Invalided.
He had not progressed beyond the rank of lieutenant during his career, but in February 1812 he was made a Commander and on 5 March 1844 he appeared on the list of retired Captains.

16 August 1846   Died at Bruges.

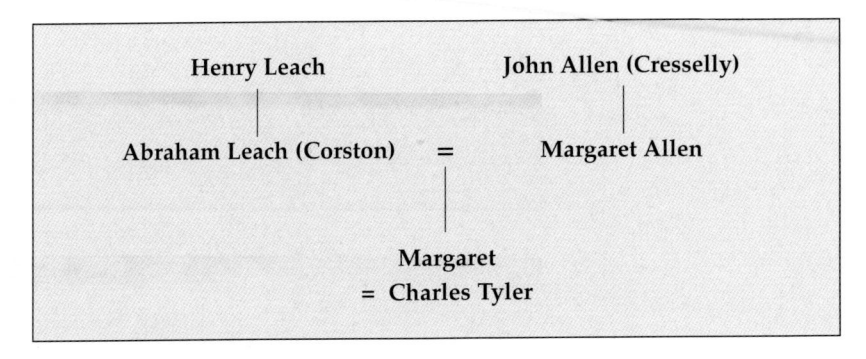

```
        Henry Leach              John Allen (Cresselly)
            |                            |
   Abraham Leach (Corston)  =     Margaret Allen
                        |
                    Margaret
                  = Charles Tyler
```

Charles Tyler married Margaret Leach in St. Mary's church, Pembroke, on 25 November 1788. Charles, aged twenty-eight, had been married before - to Mrs. Pike, widow of Captain Pike. She died leaving Charles with a son, now four years old. His second wife Margaret was of a Pembrokeshire family.

Margaret's father was an entrepreneur and landowner, also involved in lead mining. In 1780 he bought the mansion of Corston, near Castlemartin. (It remained in the family until 1936.) The bride and groom went to live at Underdown near Pembroke. They were to have six children: Ann (who married Colonel Wedgwood, Scots Guards); Caroline (married Robert Acland, of Boulston); George, the heir to the Cottrell estate; Emilia (married Colonel Mansel); Roper (married Isabel Bruce of Duffryn) and Jane (married to John Augustus Sullivan, of Richings Park, Buckinghamshire).

After their marriage, Charles Tyler was on half-pay, waiting to be assigned to a ship. Two years later he joined *Tisiphone* (one of five fireships in the navy) for a short period before going to the frigate *Maidstone* for three months. He was now a Post-Captain, a big step up in his career as it meant that he was now in command of a rated ship. The very short appointment to the *Maidstone* seems to have been a means of registering Charles as a Post-Captain, before putting him back on land, and half-pay.

Fighting the French

In 1793 Charles took command of the frigate *Meleager*. At Toulon her crew were to be involved in fierce fighting, on land as well as on water, before the British finally departed leaving the French fleet and dockyard in flames. One of Captain Tyler's junior officers was Thomas Masterman Hardy, later to become famous as captain of the *Victory* at Trafalgar and for his presence at the death of Nelson. He was to appear, ninety years later as a character in Thomas Hardy's *The Trumpet Major*.

Also on board was Midshipman George Hardinge (aged fourteen) whose uncle was George Hardinge (Attorney-General, and Justice of Glamorgan, Brecon and Radnor), who was sitting in Cardiff

TYLER

Lady Tyler, née Margaret Leach (1759-1835).

hearing the complaint against Emilia Gwinnett's gamekeeper. Later in the year, off Corsica, the French frigate *La Minerve* was sunk in San Fiorenzo Bay. George Hardinge wrote home:

> *Captain Tyler volunteered to get the frigate up again which we had sunk, and succeeded. He is to have her. She is a 40-gun frigate and her guns are 18 pounders. Her name is changed to the St. Fiorenzo.*

Fourteen years later Captain George Hardinge was to be killed in action, commanding the *St. Fiorenzo*.

83

After nearly eighteen months as captain of the frigate, Charles Tyler was given command of a larger ship, *Diadem* (64). Part of Admiral Hotham's fleet, *Diadem* and her crew were in action off Toulon again, went looking for privateers, and sailed as part of a squadron protecting merchant shipping. In a letter to his wife, Charles describes the action of 14 March 1795, and the capture of the *Ca Ira* (84) and the *Censeur* (74). He concludes:

> *Kiss my dear little ones. God grant I may soon see you and them. My best love to all my friends. I have run this over, having heard from the Admiral's Secretary if I wrote a small letter in fifteen minutes he would stuff it into his despatch, and knowing the comfort it will give you to hear I am well and tolerably happy.*

It was while holding this command that Captain Tyler charged an infantry officer (serving on *HMS Diadem*) with insubordination. Lieutenant Gerald Fitzgerald of the 11th Foot (Devonshire Regiment) was alleged to have "behaved with contempt to Captain Tyler... his superior officer when in the execution of his duty". The court-martial was convened on *Princess Royal* on 3 July 1795, the court consisting of four admirals and nine captains (including Nelson, from *Agamemnon*). Gerald Fitzgerald challenged the court's authority, arguing that a naval officer had no powers of command over an army officer. The court over-ruled him, found him guilty, and sentenced him to be sacked from the army. The case caused a furore, not only in army and naval messes, but also in government circles. The army authorities re-instated Gerald Fitzgerald, and withdrew all soldiers from ships. They were replaced by marines.

The next posting was to *L'Aigle,* a frigate which Charles joined in February 1796. His son Charles (by his first marriage) served on board as a midshipman. For the next two years *L'Aigle* cruised with some success up and down the French and Iberian coasts. There were long periods of boredom and Captain Tyler maintained discipline in the customary way: "29 July 1797. Punished Cornelius Connelly. 2 doz. (lashes) for mutiny and drunkenness".

The ship had some successes, capturing many small vessels such as the *Harriette,* taken on 12 June 1797, off the Tagus. These would have been pleasing additions to Captain Tyler's already considerable prize money. He would have been less pleased when he heard the news of a French invasion of Pembrokeshire (February 1797) only twenty miles away from his family. Fortunately, the intruders were soon rounded up, and marched off to prison.

Charles was feeling the strain, and wrote to Evan Nepean (Secretary of the Admiralty) from Spithead on 27 February 1798:

TYLER

Charles Tyler served for lengthy periods on ships patrolling the French and Spanish coasts. This is the inshore blockading squadron at Cadiz, July 1797.

My dear Sir,
Although it is many years since I have had the pleasure of seeing you, I hope you have not forgot C. Tyler who now solicits your interest for a fortnight's leave to see a sick wife at Bath. I fear she is much worse than she tells me which has shaken my resolution of not asking leave, although I have not seen my family for five years.

Charles had more to worry about five months later when *L'Aigle* was wrecked on Plane Island, off Cape Farina near Tunis. The crew, including his son, all managed to scramble ashore and were later rescued by a passing brig. The ship, considered a total loss, was set on fire to burn down to the waterline. The subsequent court martial found that Captain Tyler had not been negligent (shipwrecks of Royal Navy ships were not uncommon - eleven other ships were lost in the same year).

Charles Tyler was to command *Warrior* (74) for over four years, from February 1798. At that time the ship was with thirteen others at Cadiz - Charles had to exchange the dashing, relatively small and manoeuverable frigate for a role as part of Admiral Keith's fleet of big ships. For many months they played hide-and-seek with the French as, for example, in May 1799 when the enemy fleet came out of Brest and disappeared in a southerly direction. Keith's ships found them, eventually, off Genoa. All this took a toll of ships and men, and it became *Warrior's* turn to go home for a refit which took two months. Then back to blockading the French ports, battered by sea and wind. After one severe storm, Admiral Collingwood wrote that "The only ships that are missing from the fleet are the *Elephant* and the *Warrior*, but as both Foley and Tyler are excellent officers we have no fears whatever about them".

To the Baltic

In March 1801 Captain Charles Tyler was in the *Warrior* as part of Sir Hyde Parker's fleet sailing towards Copenhagen. The aim of the expedition was to force the Danes out of the "Armed Neutrality of the North", a pact concluded on the initiative of the Tsar and including, as well as Denmark: Prussia, Russia and Sweden. King George III was at odds with his Cabinet over the wisdom of this proposed attack on the neutral Danish navy. The King opposed it as "a very immoral act" and one which was likely to drive Denmark into Napoleon's camp (which is exactly what happened). Ignoring the King, the Cabinet members authorised the action. The Danish fleet was destroyed in harbour, but the *Warrior* took no part in this, being at anchor with the other seven ships of Parker's division.

The squadron spent April and May in the Baltic, showing the flag. On 24 April 1801 Captain Nelson wrote to Captain Tyler ("Santa Emma" is Lady Hamilton):

> *My dear Tyler*
> *Sunday the 26th being Santa Emma's birthday, I beg you*
> *will do me the favour of dining on board the St. George, as I*
> *know you are one of her votarys, and you will oblige,*
> *Your affectionate friend,*
> *Nelson*

Two months after this, Captain Charles Tyler received another letter from Nelson, this time to say that he had promoted Charles Tyler (the son) to be lieutenant on the *Alcimene*.

The *Warrior* spent most of 1801 in the Mediterranean, as the war drew to an end, before being sent off to the West Indies. Charles Tyler was in command of a small squadron *(Warrior, Bellona, Defence,* and *Zeus)* sent to find out if the French were up to anything. They were back at Spithead by July, and Captain Tyler found himself, once again, on half-pay.

Less than a year later Britain and France were at war, with the British people becoming increasingly alarmed at Napoleon Bonaparte's plans - invasion barges were being made ready in order to land about 130,000 troops, with cavalry and artillery. Charles Tyler was put in charge of his local district of *Sea Fencibles*, an organisation for coastal defence. He had about four hundred men enrolled in his district (the coast from Cardigan to Kidwelly) but had great difficulties in recruiting enough men for the tasks in hand.

Trafalgar

Although it meant leaving his family, Charles Tyler may well have welcomed the chance to get away from the over-heated world of invasion scares and back to the ordered life of a large ship of war. The sea had been, after all, his element for thirty-six years. He was called back to sea service to command *HMS Tonnant*, which was refitting at Cawsand. (His new ship had been built at Toulon, and captured at the battle of the Nile, after an extraordinarily brave resistance by her captain and crew). We have a contemporary description:

> *La Tonnant has a neat stern elegantly finished in light carved work, with "G.R." and a crown in the centre of the stern railing under the middle lantern, and her figure-head is a bust of Jupiter hurling his thunder, all beautifully executed by Mr. Dickinson and his son, the Master Carver to the Dockyard.*

Lieutenant Frederick Hoffman, who had just joined the ship, and who was to be wounded at Trafalgar, called her "this glorious ship of ships ... an equal match for any ship afloat". He also provided a vignette of the *Tonnant's* new captain:

> *Captain Tyler was from the Emerald Isle, had a slight touch of the brogue, and was replete with anecdote. He was good humoured and a gentleman, and he never punished a man unless he richly deserved it.*

The next six months were filled with familiar routine for Charles Tyler: back to the blockading of Brest and Cadiz, a cruise along the coast of Africa, and then Brest again under Admiral Collingwood. He had unwelcome news about Charles (the son from his first marriage). It came in the form of a letter from Admiral Nelson, who enclosed a copy of a report he had just sent to the Secretary of the Admiralty:

> *Lieutenant Tyler, son of that excellent and respectable officer, Captain Tyler, from an unfortunate desire to travel, and perhaps an imprudent attachment to an Italian lady, quitted the Hydra, when she was last at Malta without, I fear, the smallest inclination of ever returning to his duty on that ship.*

Nelson wrote to the *Tonnant's* captain:

> *My dear Tyler,*
> *It gives me real sorrow to be the messenger of bad news, but under the present circumstances, I hope you will think that*

> *I have done all I can to prevent your son being erased from the list of lieutenants... I still hope the young man, who does not want abilities, will recollect himself; his misfortune has been his being made independent. I will not dwell longer upon this very unpleasant subject, but be assured that I ever am, dear Tyler,*
>
> *Your most sincere friend,*
> *Nelson.*

Somehow young Charles survived six more years in the Royal Navy - with or without the Italian lady - and we hear of him serving on vessels in the West Indies and Java, until he was invalided out at the age of twenty-seven.

The battle of Trafalgar was the culmination of the Royal Navy's efforts to prevent a French invasion. After the action, the combined French and Spanish fleet had been wiped out. Britannia was able to rule the waves, especially around Europe, and a French invasion was now out of the question. Before the battle, Nelson kept his fleet (including *Tonnant*) fifty miles away from Cadiz, over the horizon. Frigates, under Captain Blackwood, kept watch on the port.

19 October 1805 9.30 a.m. Flag message from the frigates "The enemy are coming out of port". 21 October 6.00 a.m. Nelson signalled "Prepare for battle". The fleets, now in battle formation, consisted of:

	Ships	Guns	Men
British	27	2,148	17,000
French/Spanish	33	2,568	30,000

The combined fleet's formation was a long column, one ship sailing directly behind another. The British fleet was split into two lines, one led by Nelson, the other by Collingwood. The plan was that the ships of the two British lines would smash into the elongated enemy column. There was a very light wind, which blew the two British lines very slowly into the attack. Just after mid-day *Victory* (leading the "weather" column) reached the enemy. An hour-and-a-half later, Nelson was shot by a French sharpshooter.

The "lee" column of fifteen ships edged closer to the enemy. The first four ships were *Royal Sovereign* (74), *Belleisle* (74), *Mars* (74) and Charles Tyler's *Tonnant*, which had taken on extra guns to make a total of ninety. Frederick Hoffman heard bands playing on some of the ships, "Rule Britannia", and "Downfall of Paris". On his own ship, *Tonnant*, the bandsmen played "Britons strike home!". The British ships were not yet able to return fire. Benjamin Clement (son of a solicitor in Hampshire) later wrote to his father that the enemy "cut us up a good deal until we got our broadsides to bear". Some of *Tonnant's* sails were shot away. The ships of the lee division began to shoot back at noon and it would all be over by five o'clock, when only six British ships would be in a condition to continue fighting.

A broadside from the *Algeciras* killed or wounded forty of the *Tonnant's* crew, and badly damaged the rudder and stern (including Mr. Dickinson's beautifully executed carving). Lieutenant Hoffman again:

> *At length we had the honour of nestling His Majesty's ship between a French and a Spanish seventy-four, and so close that a biscuit might have been thrown on either one of them.*

Captain Tyler was hit in the right thigh by a musket ball and had to be carried below, leaving Lieutenant John Bedford in command for the rest of the fight. When the final tally came to be made, it was found that 26 of *Tonnant's* crew had been killed, and 50 wounded. This compared with 100 dead and 150 wounded on the Spanish *Monarca*.

The carnage at last stopped and *Tonnant* was found to be in such bad shape that she had to be taken in tow. A severe gale blew up, ships were dispersed, prizes lost and *Tonnant's* tow-rope parted but at last the ship was brought into harbour at Gibraltar.

Charles Tyler was laid up in Gibraltar for three weeks, and was then able to command his patched-up ship on the voyage home, in company with the *Temeraire* (the subject of Turner's famous painting). He wrote a long letter to Margaret:

> *Heaven knows how I long to once more enjoy my own fireside. I don't think I shall soon again leave it ... I shall go home by Gloucester as I don't like the ferry, it is such a walk at low water. I shall make easy journeys for I must not be out after dark.*

In a later letter he wrote:

> *My accounts for Tonnant I hope will be passed and perhaps some of the Trafalgar prize-money paid, and then we may indulge ourselves: at present the quiet country air, the society of my beloved Margaret and children will contribute a thousand times more than all the waters. I have put your ring in hand and I hope you will like it.*

In addition to the prize-money, Captain Tyler received a gold medal, a sword of honour, and the thanks of Parliament. For his wound, he was paid a government pension of £250 a year. In February 1806 he asked that an acting captain be sent to the *Tonnant* "as I am not yet able to walk without a crutch". This was done, but he seems to have kept in close touch with his ship, by letter. One of his main concerns in this year was to make sure that his son George (aged fourteen) could join the Royal Navy.

COTTRELL

BELOW:
Portsmouth was the navy's most important base. Charles Tyler was appointed "second-in-command" in April 1808, but spent very little time there. He retired from active service in November 1808.

From Cape to Cottrell

Charles Tyler was promoted to Rear-Admiral on 28 April 1808, a month before he became second-in-command at the navy's most important base, Portsmouth. The post appears to have been a nominal one only, and the nature of the new admiral's duties are not clear; they are unlikely to have been onerous. He spent very little time at the dockyard, being almost immediately detached to Portugal for five months. Ten Russian ships were bottled-up in the Tagus, and negotiations were taking place about their future. Admiral Tyler, in *Barfleur* escorted the ships to Britain, arriving on 7 October 1808. A month after his return he left Portsmouth, and active duty.

In 1810 Charles Tyler was offered a post as Admiral in Malta, but he declined. In August 1812 he was invited to take command of the tiny naval presence at the Cape of Good Hope, and this time he accepted. Cape Town had been captured from the Dutch six years earlier, and was held (a) to assist ships voyaging to India and (b) to stop the French getting their hands on it. During the years 1813-1815

TYLER

Admiral Tyler lived at Mount Nelson House, accompanied by his son George, who acted as his flag-lieutenant. In May 1813 the Admiral found time to act as steward at a subscription ball, although he was in the process of supervising the move of the naval base to Simon's Bay, thirty miles away.

When the time came to prepare for departure: his furniture was auctioned and Mount Nelson House was also sold. (It is, today, a hotel). Admiral Tyler sailed for home a few days after Christmas, 1815. He stopped at St. Helena on the way, and had a look at Napoleon Bonaparte.

Admiral Charles Tyler came to live at Cottrell in 1817 as a tenant of the Earl of Clarendon. The county of Glamorgan was changing: its population increased from 70,000 (1801) to 170,000 by 1841. The use of machinery had become more widespread, including the Melingriffith forge at Whitchurch, and the iron works at Pentyrch. The population of the Vale of Glamorgan at this time was about 14,000, that of St. Nicholas about 319. Many were becoming members of one of the non-conformist denominations, with chapels being built at Trehill and Croes-y-Parc. Even in the rural Vale, mechanisation was arriving. William Wright of St. Nicholas was awarded a prize for inventing two machines for threshing by water power (one for Mr. Evans of Fairwater, the other for Mr. Davies of Wenvoe), but in spite of the new agricultural machinery, harvest time still saw an influx of men seeking work. They came from west Wales, Somerset and Ireland, sleeping in barns and storehouses.

Some significant events for Charles and Margaret Tyler, of Cottrell:

1815 He became Admiral Sir Charles Tyler, KCB.

1824 Their daughter Emilia married Robert Mansel.
Their son George succeeded to the Cottrell estate.

1826 Jane, their youngest child, married John Augustus Sullivan.

1827 Baptism of Georgina, daughter of Robert and Emilia Mansel.

1829 Margaret's unmarried sister, Elizabeth Leach, died at Cottrell. She was sixty-seven.

1835 Margaret Tyler died at the age of seventy-six, having been married to Charles for over fifty years. A few months later Charles Tyler died at Cheltenham Spa, where he had gone for treatment to his leg.

The Cambrian wrote:

> *Sir Charles Tyler was slight in person but exceedingly good-looking; he was a very lively man and a pleasant companion, especially in the society of ladies. His manners were courteous and had all the polish of the best society.*

THE BREACH

Residents at The Breach in Sir Charles Tyler's time included:

1821	Thomas and Gwenllian Williams Sons: John and William	Labourer
	Lewis and Mary Barrett Son: Moses	Blacksmith
1822	Thomas and Susannah Rowland Son: Joseph	Carpenter
1825	William Griffith, died aged forty	
1826	James and Mary Hazel Daughter: Susan	Shepherd
1827	John and Catherine Howard Daughters: Elvira, Harriet	Labourer
1828-1841	Edward and Maria Milward Children: Anne, Jane, Maria, William, Harriet, Catherine	Labourer
1832	Edmund and Ann Miller Children: Llewellyn and Elizabeth	Labourer
1833	Morgan and Joanna Grant Children: Robert, David, Harriet	Labourer

COTTRELL LODGE

1820s	David and Catherine Dawkin and their children	Gardener

Sir George Tyler

George Tyler, who was to inherit the Cottrell estate under such peculiar circumstances, entered the Royal Naval College at the age of fourteen, joining his first ship *Lively* (38) in the winter of 1809. Like his father and half-brother, George was to survive a shipwreck in the Mediterranean but his worst experience happened nearer to home.

The thirty-eight gun *Spartan* was patrolling off the coast of Brittany when George Tyler joined her in 1810. The next year, by now a Midshipman of eighteen, he took part in a "cutting-out" expedition in Quiberon Bay. The objectives of these operations (usually done at night, and very dangerous) were to "cut out" smaller vessels in harbour, and take them away as prizes. On this raid, George lost his right arm.

He had to leave the *Spartan* to go on sick leave, and was then

TYLER

Sir George Tyler's bookplate.

attached to the *Salvador el Mundo* (captured at the battle of St. Vincent and now the flagship of Sir Robert Calder) at Portsmouth. During 1812 George Tyler served in *Hermes* (20) and *Reindeer* (18) before returning to Plymouth.

His promotion to lieutenant came just after his twenty-first birthday, in time for him to be appointed as flag-lieutenant to his father at Cape Town. On his return to Britain he was awarded a pension for the loss of his arm - £200 a year. Two years later he married Harriet Sullivan of Richings Lodge, a very elegant house near Iver, Buckinghamshire. (His sister Jane married John Augustus Sullivan, of Richings Lodge). George and Harriet were to raise ten children.

The newly-weds spent a year in East Anglia where George had been appointed "Inspecting Officer for the coast of Norfolk". There was one more sea appointment, to *Fly* (18), in which he was sent to Jersey and to Gravelines to try to resolve a dispute over oyster fisheries. At the age of thirty, George Tyler was promoted to Post rank, and placed on half-pay.

The Earl of Clarendon died in 1824, and so George at last came into his inheritance - the Cottrell estate and income became his, although his father continued to live there until his death in 1835. George Tyler was to own the estate for thirty-eight years, a period when the pace of economic and social change was accelerating: the 1830s saw not only the first Reform Act, but also the Merthyr Rising and the Chartist march on Newport; the early 1840s were the time of the Rebecca riots. One instrument of change was the boom in railway construction. The Duke of Wellington was against this, on the grounds that it would encourage the lower classes to move about. Ignoring the duke, Parliament passed the 1844 Railway Act requiring the railways to run regular trains with cheap fares. This led (as the duke had feared) to greater mobility of labour and more travel for pleasure - as well as to the growth of resorts such as Barry Island, not half-a-dozen miles from Cottrell. The main railway line to west Wales was built along the valley of the river Ely, overlooked by Cottrell House which was to find itself only one mile from a railway station (at Peterston-super-Ely) and, consequently, with easier access to almost everywhere else in Britain.

For a long period, George Tyler was mostly out of the country, not serving at sea, but as a colonial governor. Appointed Lieutenant-Governor of St. Vincent (in the Windward Islands) at the age of sixty-one, he held the post for almost eight years (from January 1833 to November 1840). The island is small (only about 130 square miles) with a forested mountain range running north-south, including Soufriere (4,094 feet), a volcano which erupted violently in 1821, 1902 and 1979. A British settlement was established in 1762 and, in 1765, a botanical garden was set up, the first in the western hemisphere. A Carib uprising had been put down in 1795, and many were deported; for extra security Fort Charlotte was built in the capital, Kingstown. George Tyler's tenure was at a significant time for the people of Britain and the colonies because, in 1834, slavery was abolished.

George Tyler was knighted in 1838. In that and the following year detailed surveys were made of the Cottrell estate for the purposes of the Tithe Commutation Act, 1836, which allowed payment of church tithes to be commuted to a rent-charge (based on the price of corn). The beneficiary of the tithes in the parish of St. Nicholas was the rector, the Reverend Roper Trevor Tyler, Sir George's brother. Sir George was away governing St. Vincent, so Cottrell House and 128 acres were occupied by Roper Tyler. There were fifty other tenants, some renting many acres, others small cottages.

Three years later a census was taken which gives us an accurate list of those at Cottrell House on 6 June 1841. Those present, in addition to the servants, included Sir George and Lady Tyler; their children Harriet Georgina (20), Anne Marie (18), Charles Frederick (15), Caroline (11), Edward (10), John (9), Louise (8), St. Vincent (6); Sir George's sister and her husband (Jane and John Sullivan) and their children Roper (14), Emilia (9), Frederick (6) and James (4). Among the servants was Marie Baklin, a "lady's maid" from France.

In the year of the Great Exhibition (1851), Sir George Tyler became a Member of Parliament, and served for five years. He was well known for his die-hard opposition to free trade, as was his fellow county member, C.R. Mansel Talbot.

THE BREACH

Some of the residents during the time of Sir George Tyler:

1838	Philip and Susan Griffith	Labourer
	Son: William	
1839	Llewellyn David, aged four months, died.	
	David and Mary Jenkins	Labourer
	Children: David, Ann, William	
	Samuel and Elvira Griffiths	Labourer
	Children: Daniel, Charles, Edwin, Matilda, William	
1843-1852	John and Anne Thomas	Labourer/Gamekeeper
	Children: Thomas, John, James (died) James, Edwin, William.	
1851	Samuel and Charlotte Humphrey	
	Children: John, William, Mary, Sarah Ann.	
	Samuel and his two boys were labourers on the estate.	
1861	Thomas and Amy James	Woodcutter
	Children: John, Mary, Eliza.	
	James and Agnes Hewitt	Shepherd
	They came from Devon.	
	Children: Agnes (a servant), William, Mary (farm servant)	
	Grandson: Isaac.	

THE LODGE

1835	Elizabeth Large died, aged fifty-two.	
1839	David and Mary Jenkins	Labourer
	(formerly of 'The Breach')	
	Mary's mother, described as a pauper, was living with them.	
1848	James and Margaret Morgan	Gamekeeper
	Daughter: Margaret.	
1854	John and Anne Keel	Gardener
	Their son died, aged three months.	
1861	Edward and Ann Taylor	Labourer
	They came from Wiltshire.	

COTTRELL

David Vaughan

Sir George (as a sailor, colonial governor and parliamentarian) needed a reliable agent at Cottrell. David Vaughan was the man. Architect, surveyor, and father of twenty-two children: David Vaughan was also the Cottrell estate manager. He built up an extensive architectural practice, building Bonvilston House (and its Lodge, which still stands), Fairwater House, and drawing up plans in 1856 for the National Provincial Bank in Cowbridge. His biggest project was Bridgend Town Hall, which was demolished in 1971. David Vaughan repaired and renovated several local churches including those at Llanharry, Michaelston-super-Ely, and St. Nicholas. He was surveyor for the new river bridge (1858-59) at Peterston-super-Ely. (His name is still visible - just - on a commemorative plaque.)

David Vaughan was also responsible for the enlargement of Cottrell House. He added a storey and two big wings, although one wing was not built until fifteen or so years later. His journals record some of his activities in running the Cottrell estate - a frequent entry reads, simply, *"Over the Cottrell estate"*. More specifically, he was responsible for the collection of rents (twice a year); the supervision of accounts; the letting of land; keeping an eye on thatching and timber-felling; and construction and drainage. The range of his activities may be seen from these journal samples, taken from the 1840s and 1850s.

15 December 1842 At Cottrell surveying for altering the house and improvements.

17 July 1856 At St. Fagans with Mr. Llewellyn over the Cottrell land called Ely Rise.

In August and September he was with the "mineral surveyors" looking for coal at Cwm Cuke.

30 October 1856 With Sir George Tyler about his kennel, etc.

3 December 1857 At St. Fagans over Sir George Tyler's land, respecting exchanging with the Hon. Mr. Clive.

23 December 1857 Distributing Admiral Sir George Tyler's beef to the poor.

David Vaughan had ten children by his first wife, Harriet Rees of Welsh St. Donats. Eight years after her death he married the young Anne Day, who produced twelve more, the last when David Vaughan was seventy-one.

Sir George Tyler died in 1862, leaving his widow to live on at Cottrell for another eleven years. A census was taken in 1871 (2nd April) which recorded seven family members, looked after by fourteen staff. The "head of household" was given as Lady Tyler (Sir George's widow). Also present were her unmarried daughter Anna M. Tyler

(49) and "Harriet D.A. Richards" (aged 13) - her father had died before she was born and her mother (Lady Tyler's daughter) had married again, to Pierpont H. Mundy present at Cottrell and listed as Lady Tyler's son-in-law, as well as "Major-General". His sons, Harriet Richards's step-brothers, were also staying in the house.

The employees included: Puis Henn (47) the German butler, and Marie Jones (a widow of 63), the housekeeper. As well as a Swiss governess there were a lady's maid, cook, nurse, two housemaids, a nursery maid, kitchen maid, scullery maid, footman, and a groom.

George Henry Tyler

Lady Tyler died on 25 July 1873, to be succeeded by her son, George, who was aged forty-nine. George Henry Tyler had purchased his commission in the 13th Regiment of Foot (later the Somerset Light Infantry) at the age of eighteen. He was with the 1st Battalion in India from 1842 to 1845, when it returned to Britain (to Walmer, in Kent). The battalion went to Ireland in 1847, remaining there for four years before being sent to Gibraltar. The next move was in 1855 when the 1st Battalion, and Captain Tyler, sailed to the Crimea. He was at the battle of Tchernaya and at the siege of Sebastopol, being awarded the Crimea campaign medal and the Imperial Order of the 5th Class (Turkish) of the Legion of Honour.

The battalion returned to Gibraltar, but was soon off again - back to India, after twelve years away. It was dispatched from Gibraltar in haste in the aftermath of the Indian Mutiny, arriving in October 1857. The soldiers were in India during the period when the British army's actions have been described as "indiscriminate ferocity" and "merciless vengeance". Major G.H. Tyler was awarded the Indian Mutiny campaign medal. He retired from the army in April 1859, selling his commission and being granted the rank of Brevet Lieutenant-Colonel.

George Henry Tyler was to live for only five years after inheriting Cottrell. In his will he bequeathed the estate to his brother Gwinnett for life, and then to his nephew George William Tyler (eldest son of Frederick, deceased brother of George Henry and Gwinnett).

Gwinnett Tyler

His first name celebrated Emilia Gwinnett, who left Cottrell to his father. The house had now been lived in by the Tyler family since Gwinnett Tyler's grandfather (Charles) moved in over seventy years before. Gwinnett Tyler was also a naval man and in 1848 was under fire in Nicaragua. (The details were reported in the *London Gazette*).

Two British subjects had been abducted by Colonel Salas of the Nicaraguan army, so Admiral Sir Francis Austen sent off two vessels to deal with the matter - *HMS Alarm* (26) and *HMS Vixen* (6 guns, and described as a "steam sloop"). A force of 260 men set off up the River San Juan de Nicaragua. They were in twelve boats taken from the two ships, the young Gwinnett Tyler being in the *Alarm's* barge which contained a crew of thirteen, ten marines and a 12-pounder gun. Their destination was a post at Serapaqui about thirty miles up the river, which was very fast flowing and contained several rapids. After pulling on their oars against this current for seventy-two hours, the leading boat came under fire, but the force had to carry on rowing for another hour and forty minutes before being able to land. Ten minutes later they were in command of the fort and Stoker Dennis Burke had captured the enemy's colours.

Nine prisoners were taken, arms and ammunition were thrown into the river, and the post was set on fire. Two of the attackers were killed, and thirteen wounded (three from Gwinnett Tyler's boat). Mr. Tyler was among those Captain Loch wished to recommend to the Admiral's "favourable notice". The fate of the kidnapped British subjects was not recorded.

Gwinnett Tyler served subsequently as a lieutenant on *HMS Leander* (1850-1852), but left the Royal Navy in 1853 having refused to take up an appointment on the *Philomel*. He married Judith Parry of Mount Gernos (Cardiganshire) and did not live at Cottrell. The St. Nicholas Poor Rate records for 1879 and 1880 show Cottrell as owned by Gwinnett Tyler, but occupied by his niece, the twenty-two year old Harriet Diana Arabella Mary Richards.

George William Tyler

George William Tyler (nephew of George Henry Tyler and Gwinnett Tyler) inherited Cottrell in 1886, but did not live there. Born in 1852, he was another sea-going Tyler, entering as a naval cadet just before his fourteenth birthday. He served for over twenty years, but his career was a chequered one: in 1870 he was a month late joining his ship and two years later was fined one month's pay for misconduct. By January 1885 he was with the Naval Brigade on the Nile - part of the expedition trying to get up the river to rescue Gordon, besieged in Khartoum.

General Sir Garnet Wolseley appointed his naval aide - Lord Charles William Delapoer Beresford - to command the Naval Brigade. Eight hundred flat-bottomed boats were built and nearly 400 Canadian "voyageurs" were hired. Eight steam pinnaces and two paddle steamers were fitted out. By the time G.W. Tyler joined the Brigade, at Gubat, it had been involved in fierce fighting in the desert, all the other officers were *hors de combat* and Lord Charles Beresford was so ill that he could not walk. By now Khartoum had fallen, and Gordon was

TYLER

BELOW:
Cottrell House in the late nineteenth century. Compare this with the illustration on page 72.

dead. Thirty thousand Dervishes were making for Gubat, so the Naval Brigade (and the rest of the force) decamped - heavily laden and, in some cases, without shoes. They eventually reached the safety of the fort at Abu Klea, where the Naval Brigade was broken up and the men posted back to their ships.

Mr. Tyler and Lord Charles Beresford did not get on. Lord Charles reported to the Admiralty on Lieutenant Tyler's "want of due energy and alacrity" and the fact that he "did not perform his duty in a strict and officer-like manner". George William Tyler requested permission to retire from the service (he had just inherited Cottrell) but this was refused. Six months later he was out - on medical grounds - and commuted his pension for a sum of (in today's terms) about £120,000. He sold Cottrell to his cousin, Harriet, who had lived there for some years.

Harriet Diana Arabella Mary Richards

Harriet Richards arrived in the world seven months after her father died. She was born at Cottrell and continued to live there as a young girl. Her mother, Harriet Georgina Tyler (eldest child of Sir George Tyler) married Edward Priest Richards:

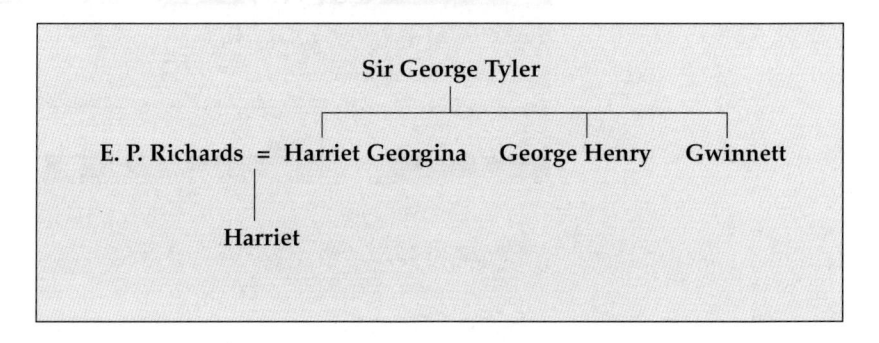

```
                        Sir George Tyler
            ┌──────────────────┼──────────────┬──────────┐
E. P. Richards = Harriet Georgina    George Henry    Gwinnett
                |
             Harriet
```

Edward Priest Richards, Harriet's husband, was a great-nephew of another Edward Priest Richards, who was agent for the Marquess of Bute's estates in South Wales. The Richards family were very influential in Cardiff, and the elder E.P. Richards has been described as its most powerful citizen. Very wealthy, unmarried, he lived on his Plasnewydd estate. The younger Edward Priest Richards married Harriet Georgina Tyler on 5 February 1856. Within two years he was dead, thrown from his horse in Plwcca Lane (now City Road), Cardiff. His daughter Harriet - born after his death - was to inherit a fortune (and the Plasnewydd estate) from Edward Priest Richards, the elder. A very wealthy young woman, she married a Scottish laird.

7. Mackintosh

ABOVE:
Cottrell House, 1930's.

The Mackintosh of Mackintosh

Harriet Diana Arabella Mary Richards married Alfred Donald Mackintosh of Mackintosh (28th Chief of Clan Mackintosh) on 14 April 1880 (having signed a comprehensive "Ante-Nuptial Contract of Marriage" the day before).

Alfred's immediate forebears were fur traders: his grandfather (25th Chief) had gone to Detroit as a young man and his son, Alfred's father (26th Chief) joined the business. The next Chief was Aeneas (Alfred's elder brother) who succeeded to the title at the age of fourteen. He later enlarged the family seat Moy Hall (Inverness-shire) in the Scottish Baronial style before marrying a sister of the Duchess of Montrose.

Alfred Donald Mackintosh was born at Moy and sent away to school at Brighton, and to Cheltenham College. The next step was the Royal Military College Sandhurst, where he was a "Gentleman Cadet", and then (1870) a commission in the 71st Regiment (Highland Light Infantry). Alfred served with his battalion in Gibraltar and Malta, being promoted to Lieutenant, and serving as adjutant for a time.

Meanwhile, back in Scotland the 27th Chief - Alfred's brother -

101

had died. His baby, born after his death, turned out to be a girl, which meant that the Chieftainship and the Moy estates passed to Alfred, then serving in Malta. This unexpected turn of events impelled Alfred to resign from the regular army, although he transferred immediately to the reserve force, becoming a Captain in the militia battalion of his local regiment, the Cameron Highlanders. He had been "The Mackintosh" for four years when he married Harriet Richards. The pair lived half of the year at Cottrell and the other half at Moy - with time out for the "season" (especially Ascot) when they stayed at their town house: 8 Hill Street, Mayfair.

THE MACKINTOSH

Clan Chiefs used to be known as (e.g.) "Mackintosh of that Ilk". According to the family, the correct usage is: "The Mackintosh of Mackintosh" or, in shortened form, "The Mackintosh". (Friends of the 28th Chief called him "Alfie".)

Spelling: the name has been written in a variety of ways over the years, including "McIntosh" - the man who killed Button Gwinnett. The Chiefs have used the form "Mackintosh" for over two hundred years.

Clan Chattan: The Mackintosh was also Chief of Clan Chattan, a confederation of septs, which included Clans Mackintosh, Macpherson, Shaw, Macbean, Farquharson, Phail, Davidson, MacGillivray, MacQueen, Macthomas, MacLeans of Dochgarroch, MacIntyres of Badenoch.

Moy Hall is about eight hundred feet above sea level, surrounded by hills, and endures severe weather in winter - cold, wet and, often, snow. In 1896 a railway halt was built at Moy, making the transportation of people, animals and effects to Cottrell a much simpler task. Alfred and Harriet's main pre-occupation at Cottrell was hunting; at Moy, fishing and shooting. Shooting was, in fact, a major source of income for the Mackintosh estates. It was on a large scale - for example in 1910 at Moy 8,178 grouse were shot; in 1913 at Coignafearn, 5,000 grouse and 86 stags; in 1935, at Meallmore, 5,400 grouse. In 1912, at Moy alone, 17,436 birds and animals were killed, of well over a dozen species.

BELOW:
Moy Hall, Inverness-shire in about 1899.
The Mackintoshes spent their summers here and their winters at Cottrell.

THE MACKINTOSH ESTATES

Moy	11,000 acres
Meallmore	9,475
Daviot	5,140
Tordaroch	1,720
Coignafearn	39,000
Glenspean	23,258
Glenroy	8,825
*Dunachton	10,774
Glenfeshie	5,500
Dalcross	1,058
	115,750

* Sold in 1937, after being in the family for five hundred years.

Cottrell

The world of commerce and industry was closing in on Cottrell. For south Wales, the period from 1880 until the First World War was a boom time. Economic activity was increasing, and an infrastructure of railways and ports was being developed - in July 1889 Barry Dock was opened, only five miles away from Cottrell. The Great Western main line, and the Barry Railway sidings at Peterston carried the sounds of the industrializing world to the peaceful estate.

The population of Cardiff increased by 250 per cent during the last two decades of the century, which brought demands for a greater variety of education, sports and entertainment. In 1883 the University opened in the Old Infirmary (large crowds thronged the town for the occasion and the bells of St. John's church rang all day). On 8 October 1878 the Theatre Royal in St. Mary Street opened with W.S. Gilbert's **Pygmalion and Galatea** to be followed by Buffalo Bill's **Wild West Show**, Oscar Wilde's **A Woman of No Importance** and Dr. Joseph Parry's operas **Blodwen, Arianwen** and **Silvia**. The New Theatre opened in December 1906. The "golden age" of Welsh rugby was approaching (1900 - 1912) and the Triple Crown was won six times.

Roath

Building houses at Roath ensured that the Mackintoshes could keep up their affluent style of life. Developments in Cardiff made Mrs. Mackintosh's Plasnewydd estate a prime site. Fields were disappearing under roads and houses and in 1883 Cardiff Town Council offered to buy fifty acres of Plasnewydd for use as a public park. This set the landowner thinking, and plans were ordered up for a "development" of terraced houses: 2750 dwellings on a hundred acres with a population of about 13,000, the whole thing taking about seventeen years, from 1884 to 1901. The street names chosen all had Mackintosh connections: for example, Mackintosh Place, Inverness Place, Arabella Street, Donald Street, Moy Road, and Cottrell Road. The mansion of Plasnewydd was now of no use to the Mackintoshes so, in 1890, they gave it - with two acres - to the inhabitants of the new houses, to be used for recreational pursuits. It exists today as the Mackintosh Institute.

What all this meant to Alfred and Harriet was that, from 1885 onwards, they could rely on a very large and increasing income from ground rents, in addition to all their other sources of income.

The Mackintoshes continued to divide their time between Mayfair, Moy and Cottrell. For the first half-dozen years of their married life they lived at Cottrell, but did not own it. The succession of owners looks like this:

1862 - 1873   Lady Tyler (widow of Sir George)

MACKINTOSH

1873 - 1878   George Henry Tyler
1878 - 1886   Gwinnett Tyler
1878-1880   Tenant: Miss Richards
1880   Miss Richards becomes Mrs. Mackintosh
1881   Tenants: The Mackintoshes
1886   Gwinnett Tyler died, and the estate passed to George William Tyler, who sold it to his cousin, Mrs. Mackintosh.

Country houses and agricultural estates were not flourishing at this time and G.W. Tyler was probably very happy to sell out to his cousin. The first two stages of the Plasnewydd housing project had been completed, so she could easily afford it. Some public documents (e.g. census returns, and the Poor Rate accounts) show the owner of Cottrell as being "The Mackintosh". The real situation seems to have been that he owned the Scottish estates and Mrs. Mackintosh owned Cottrell. (The Married Women's Property Act 1882 had made this feasible, as it gave married women the right to separate ownership of property.) We can now sum up the Tylers' long involvement with the estate:

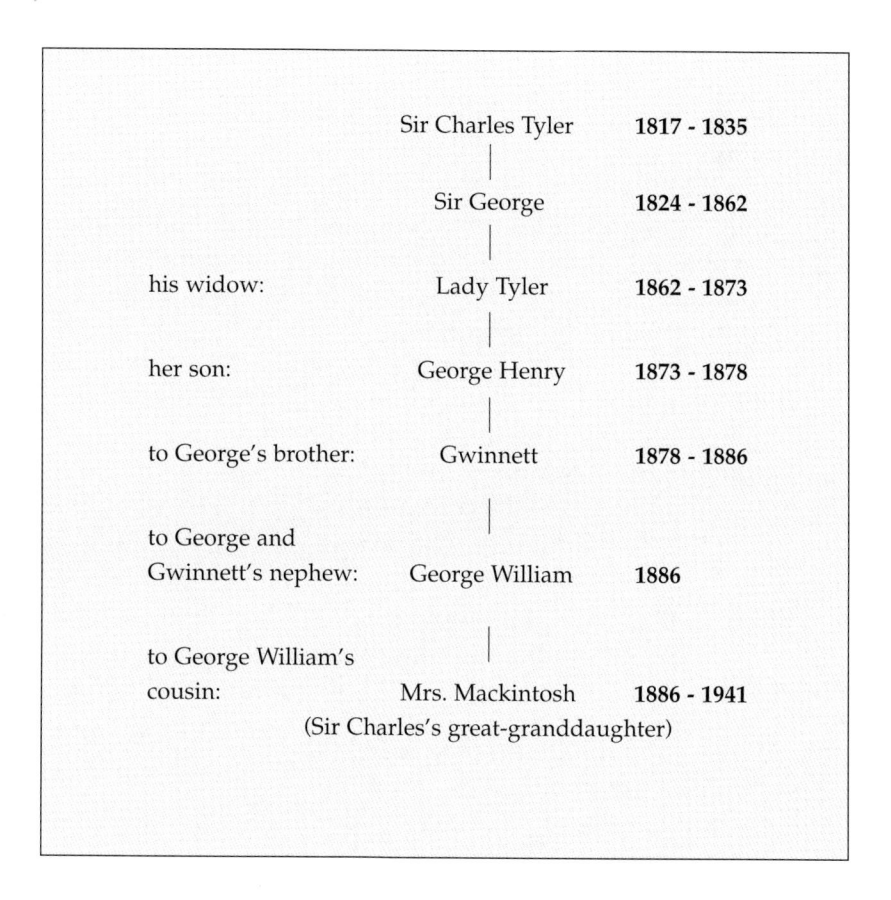

	Sir Charles Tyler	1817 - 1835
	Sir George	1824 - 1862
his widow:	Lady Tyler	1862 - 1873
her son:	George Henry	1873 - 1878
to George's brother:	Gwinnett	1878 - 1886
to George and Gwinnett's nephew:	George William	1886
to George William's cousin:	Mrs. Mackintosh	1886 - 1941
	(Sir Charles's great-granddaughter)	

The Glamorgan Hunt at Cottrell in 1901. Both Mackintoshes were keen riders to hounds and supporters of the Hunt, of which The Mackintosh became Master.

Hunting

The Glamorgan Hunt was not large, as hunts went in the 1880s. The fashionable packs in the Shires were much bigger: the Cottesmore had 60 couple of hounds, the Quorn 55 and the Pytchley, 54. The Glamorgan was around half their size, rubbing along with about 28 couple, with names like **Beatrice, Legacy, Traveller, Termagent, Trickster, Sentiment, Surety,** and **Slanderer.** It was, nonetheless, very well supported by what the local papers tended to refer to as "the elite of the county". The Mackintosh was an enthusiast, and was Master from 1897 to 1906.

In spite of house building and industrialisation there were still great tracts of open country to ride over. Thus on 28 January 1882 The Mackintosh attended a meet at Llanishen (now a densely populated suburb) which was described as "a rural hamlet". There were over two hundred on horseback and a crowd on foot.

The Mackintoshes supported the hunt steeplechases and point-to-point races. There is a record of the Glamorgan Hunt Steeplechases in April 1884 at Penlline, when there were nine runners in the **Red Coat Race** for a cup presented by Mrs. Mackintosh. Her husband's horse

Torpedo came second in the Open Hunters' Steeplechase, of about three miles. Almost thirty years later (1912) The Mackintosh was still involved, acting as Starter in the races held at Bonvilston.

The Hunt Ball was the social event of the year. In January 1882 it was held in the Cardiff Assembly Rooms, with lavish decorations by "Messrs. Howell & Co., St. Mary Street" - "The windows were hung with scarlet baize, white muslin curtains, and Chinese lanterns. Between each window there was an elegant pier glass in an ebony frame, trimmed with white drapery and surmounted with a stag's head" - from the Mackintosh estates?. Alfred and Harriet would have waltzed, and performed "The Lancers" to tunes from **The Mikado** and **Ruddigore.** The polkas listed on the dance card were **Buffalo Bill, Bugle Call** and **Hanky Panky** and even more energetic were the "Galops" **Post Horn** and **John Peel.**

The social round also included dinners. One (men only), at the Bear in Cowbridge involved not only eating, but enduring several speeches and drinking **ten** toasts. No wonder some of those present were reported to have "indulged in harmony".

In 1881 The Mackintosh was twenty-nine. Mrs. Mackintosh was twenty-three. The census taken on 3 April lists their daughter Violet, who was only eight weeks old. (She was destined to die two years later.) Puis Henn, the butler, is still there (as ten years ago) but is now a British citizen. Maria Jones, aged seventy-three, is still housekeeper. One new face is Hugh Fraser, The Mackintosh's piper. There are fifteen staff, including two nurses.

Five months later, we hear of Mrs. Mackintosh presenting two new bells to the parish church of St. Nicholas. She also paid for "rehanging and re-clappering" the old bells, repairing the wooden frame, and for a new "chiming apparatus": The two new bells were each inscribed "Presented by Ella Mackintosh of Mackintosh - 1881".

Two years after their daughter's death, an heir to the Mackintosh estates was born (at Moy, on 6 August 1885) and named Angus Alexander.

There were lavish celebrations at Moy when he arrived at his twenty-first birthday in 1906, and he looked set to become the 29th Chief. Like his father, he chose an army career, joining the Royal Horse Guards (The Blues) for a period of service which included a year spent in Ireland as aide-de-camp to the commander-in-chief, Sir Arthur Paget. He was there during what was, as so often, a troubled time: there were strikes, gun-running, and more para-military forces were coming into being with names such as the Ulster Volunteer Force, the Citizen Army, and the Irish Volunteers. In March 1914 there was the "mutiny" of army officers at the Curragh. The Great War began five

> **ANGUS ALEXANDER MACKINTOSH**
> **(Son of Alfred and Harriet)**
>
> Born 6 August 1885 at Moy
>
> | | |
> |---|---|
> | 4 July 1906 | Probationary Officer in the Household Cavalry (The Blues) |
> | 5 July 1908 | Lieutenant |
> | 22 September 1913 | A.D.C. to the Commander-in-Chief of British forces in Ireland |
> | 6 October 1914 | To Flanders with the British Expeditionary Force |
> | 30 October 1914 | Wounded |
> | 8 December 1914 | Transferred to U.K. |
> | November 1915 | A.D.C. to Governor-General, Canada |
> | 3 November 1917 | Married Lady Maud Cavendish in Ottawa Cathedral |
> | 14 October 1918 | Died of pneumonia in Washington |
>
> His daughter was born two weeks before his death.
> She was baptized: "Anne Peace Arabella"

months later and Angus was sent to Flanders with his regiment. Wounded after three weeks, he was brought home and sent off to be A.D.C. to the Governor-General of Canada, (the Duke of Devonshire), whose daughter he married. Angus died in October 1918, aged thirty-three. His daughter was born a fortnight before his death.

The Mackintosh made his own contribution to the war effort by taking command, at the age of sixty-three, of the training depot at Invergordon, which housed the 3rd (Special Reserve) Battalion of the Cameron Highlanders. (Alfred Mackintosh had retained his links with the militia, rising from Honorary Major in 1886 to Colonel in 1897. He had retired on Christmas Eve 1902.)

Mrs. Mackintosh was President of the Inverness County Branch of the Red Cross from 1907 to 1937 and during the war organised and financed an auxiliary military hospital - Hedgefield House, Inverness - which had twenty-four beds and admitted "other ranks".

MACKINTOSH

The Recollections of Charles Deere of Bonvilston

The *"Recollections of Charles Deere"* were produced in typescript by the Bonvilston Society in about 1984. Mr. Deere, then in his eighty-seventh year, was able to provide a fascinating account of village life in the early part of the twentieth century. Some parts of the work relate to Cottrell:

"I can remember the following staff employed at Cottrell -

A butler, two footmen, a hallboy, a valet and piper, a handyman, two chauffeurs, a coachman (before they had motor cars), four grooms, three or four gardeners, a farm bailiff, two farm workers, an estate mason, a mason's help, an estate carpenter, a gamekeeper, a housekeeper, a cook, a lady's maid, a laundress, two kitchen maids, two housemaids".

"The married staff all had cottages, rent free, on the estate. Single grooms lived above the saddle room and single gardeners in a bothy in the gardens. The wages were, of course, in those days very low - ... (but) cottages were rent free and there was free milk, for those living out, and some of the men had a tailor-made suit of clothes bought for them every year."

"The piper valet was a Mr. Macdonald, a real Scottie. He was with The Mackintosh for many years. He would march to and fro in front of the house from 7.30 to 8 in the morning and also in the evening, when dinner was being served." (Duncan Macdonald lived at The Breach).

"During the winter there would be about four organised shoots on the Cottrell estate. Local men and boys were asked to go out to help."

"Every year when coming from Scotland, the household brought enough live sheep to last them through the winter. The sheep were let loose on Cottrell Park and killed on the farm as they were needed."

"The Mackintosh had a large engine installed in a building on the estate and this made the electricity for the house and buildings. It was there when I was a small boy and this is the first I remember of electric light."

"Cottrell Mansion had its own water supply, which was pumped up from a well or spring about half a mile away. There was a curling pond in the wood which was, of course, only of use in the frosty weather. The Mackintosh played and took some of the staff to join in the games. There was also a fishpond made in the wood and stocked with trout and other fish."

BELOW:
King, Prime Minister and Mackintosh at Moy in September 1921. King George V had asked Lloyd George (on holiday in Scotland) to come to see him to discuss the content of a letter to be sent to Eamon de Valera. Changes were made to the draft, which was approved at a special Cabinet meeting in Inverness. Talks with the Irish delegates were resumed, and agreement was reached, setting up an Irish Free State, as a Dominion within the Commonwealth.

"(The Mackintoshes) were very good to everyone and at Christmas time gave joints of beef and coal to the poorer people. The school children of St. Nicholas and Bonvilston were treated to a Christmas party every year. This included cakes and tea, a bag of sugared almonds, a dip in the bran tub, and a march around the Christmas tree, and everyone was given a nice present. It was a very large tree standing in the coach-house and always very beautifully decorated and lit up with numerous candles. Proceedings would end up with the National Anthem and three cheers for The Mackintosh and Mrs. Mackintosh, called for by the schoolmaster of St. Nicholas - Mr. Coles."

The Mackintoshes gave the Bonvilston "Reading Room" to the village, as a social centre, and also donated a cricket pavilion. They started a Boy Scout troop, paying for uniforms and equipment, and providing

Cottrell House, 1930's.

an old cottage for meetings. Charles Deere writes, also, that "there was good grouse shooting and fishing around Moy Hall. King George V was entertained there several times and he, like the Mackintoshes, was an excellent shot with the gun."

King George V was a friend of Alfred Mackintosh, staying at Moy on a number of occasions. He was there in the September of 1921 when a critical point was reached in negotiations between the British government and Irish delegates. Talks had been suspended, and the Cabinet view was that Eamon de Valera was responsible. The King saw the draft of a letter to be sent by the Prime Minister to de Valera, and thought it too brusque, so Lloyd George (also on holiday in the Highlands) was invited over to Moy. The Prime Minister agreed to make changes to the text of the letter, which was then approved at a special Cabinet meeting held in Inverness. The Irish talks were

Cottrell House, 1930's.

resumed and an agreement was reached setting up the Irish Free State.

At Moy, the King met The Mackintosh's small grand-daughter. "What is your name?" he asked. "I'm Anne Peace Arabella Mackintosh of Mackintosh", she replied. "Ah!" said the King, "I'm just plain George!"

The Mackintosh held several public positions, ranging from that of Lord-Lieutenant of Inverness-shire to President of the Highland Agricultural Society, instituting shows at Moy. The Freedom of Inverness was conferred on him in 1925.

In 1930, tenants and employees of both Moy and Cottrell gathered to celebrate Alfred and Harriet's golden wedding, making presentations of gold plate to the couple. Travel between Moy and Cottrell had become much easier over the years, and was usually now by means of a private railway carriage coupled to a normal time-tabled train. People, animals and impedimenta could be stowed on board at Moy and be taken off at Peterston station, a few minutes away from Cottrell. On one occasion, however, attaching The Mackintosh's carriage led to an accident. The station-master of Peterston-super-Ely stated at the subsequent Inquiry that this manoeuvre took place once a year (with a passenger coach) and about six times a year with horse boxes.

On 13 June 1936 the manoeuvring had been completed and the Mackintosh party went on its way, now part of a main-line train. The

MACKINTOSH

BELOW:
Cottrell House interiors, during the 1930's.

engine which had shunted the special coach was still on the main line when it was hit by another passenger train. Both engines and four coaches were derailed, damaging 120 yards of track and injuring twelve passengers and the engine drivers. The Mackintosh party, oblivious to all this, was speeding northwards.

Problems could arise, also, on the roads. There was not much traffic but what there was could, even in the 1920s, be a nuisance on the narrow lanes of the Vale of Glamorgan. The Mackintosh complained to Police Sergeant Hamilton about an incident involving dangerous driving. On 8 May 1929 there was a motor-cycle "Reliability run" up the lane between Croes-y-Parc and Kingsland. The Mackintosh, Mrs. Mackintosh, Mr. and Mrs. C.K. Cory (of Kingsland) and some others were walking along the lane when five motor-bikes came roaring round the corner "and the whole of the party who were walking on the

113

COTTRELL

The Mackintoshes, 1930's.

lane had to get up on the bank out of the way" - not easy for the septuagenarians in the group.

During the Thirties, Mrs. Mackintosh continued with her charitable and social work. She was particularly involved with the St. John Ambulance organisation, being "Lady President" of the Glamorgan Centre and a member of the headquarters committee of the Priory. She supported, financially and in other ways, the **Medical Comforts** scheme. This was adopted in Cardiff in the 1920s with depots being set up to provide those in need with hot-water bottles, air cushions, water beds, thermometers, invalid chairs and clothing for babies. Before long, depots were set up in all parts of Wales, and local authorities were providing rooms for storage, supervised by St. John's nursing members. Accident cases came in, and home visits were made. All help and advice was free. Money was raised by whist drives, fetes, and garden parties, the major social event being the annual garden party at Cottrell.

In recognition of her efforts, Mrs. Mackintosh was promoted in the St. John hierarchy from 'Dame of Grace' to 'Dame of Justice', her

BELOW:
Queen Mary at Cottrell in 1938. She had driven over from St. Fagans where she was staying with the Plymouths.
Standing (left to right):
Sir Gerald Chichester (the Queen's private secretary); Lady Cynthia Colville; Lord Stanmore; the Earl of Plymouth; Alberta, the dowager Countess of Plymouth; Lord George Wellesley; Joseph Jones (Chief Constable of Glamorgan).
Seated (left to right:
The Countess of Plymouth; Mrs. Mackintosh; Queen Mary; The Mackintosh; Anne Peace Arabella Mackintosh (grand-daughter).

sponsors being the Earl and Countess of Plymouth, Lady Bute and Morgan Lindsey. The Prior - the Prince of Wales - flew from Windsor Great Park to Cardiff in his own Vickers monoplane (which had cost him £10,000). After a service in St. John's church, Mrs. Mackintosh and others were invested at a ceremony in City Hall.

Alfred Mackintosh had only two months of life left when he donned his Lord-Lieutenant's uniform to take the salute at a ceremonial parade of the Camerons in Inverness. He died on 14 November 1938 and was buried in the family vault at Petty, near Moy. His piper played "Mackintosh's Lament". Alfred and Harriet had been married for over fifty-eight years. She was to live without him for another two years, in increasingly poor health, and having to take shelter from bombing raids.

By 1939 the Luftwaffe had dossiers providing bombing information for all likely targets in Britain - Cottrell and the surrounding countryside appear on a photograph taken by a German reconnaissance aeroplane early in the war. This frail old lady, in a blacked-out Cottrell House would have realised that she was surrounded by targets - docks, the main railway line and sidings, and various military installations. For Cottrell there was a special hazard.

Particulars

LOT 1
(Coloured Purple on Plan No. 1)

The Residential Estate
with
The Mansion House
known as
"COTTRELL"

GARDENS, GROUNDS, PARKLANDS, ENTRANCE LODGE, COTTAGES, WOODLANDS,

AND

THE FARM AND LANDS

known as

"Gwreiddyn"

the whole containing

194.656 Acres
(or thereabouts)

"COTTRELL" is approached by means of a drive from the Cardiff-Cowbridge Road. There are also two back drives leading to the Peterston-super-Ely Road.

The Accommodation comprises :

On Ground Floor.

Entrance Porch ; Hall (40' 6" x 19") (Oak panelled) ; Cloak Room and Lavatory ; Library (35' x 18' 6") ; Ante Room (17' x 18'), Large Drawing Room (32' x 17') ; Small Drawing Room (24' 6" x 17') ; Dining Room (35' 6" x 21') ; Morning Room (17' 6" x 18') ; Gun Room (17' 6" x 10') ; Billiard Room (34' x 20') ; Housekeepers' Room ; Butler's Pantry ; Servants' Hall ; Kitchen ; Scullery and Offices ; Cellarage in Basement.

On First Floor.

South Bedroom (21' x 18' 6") ; Dressing Room (13' x 18' 6") ; Pink Bedroom (14' x 17') and Dressing Room ; Yellow Room (18' x 14') ; South East Bedroom and Dressing Room ; Bathroom and W.C. ; Maids' Bedroom ; Linen Room, Store Room, Housemaids' Pantry and W.C. ; West Bedroom (15' x 16') ; Bathroom and W.C. ; Moy Bedroom (15' x 12' 6") ; Blue Bedroom (18' 6" x 18') ; School Room (18' x 17' 6") ; School Bedroom (17' x 10' 6") ; three Secondary Bedrooms.

On Second Floor.

Three Bedrooms ; Maids' Workroom (14' x 18') ; five Staff Bedrooms, and Bathroom and W.C.

At rear of house, with covered way from house : Boot Hole, Bake-house, Dairy, Kitchen, Valets' Room, with five Bedrooms over.

Game Larder, Ash Tip, two Loose Boxes with Groom's Rooms over approached by outside Staircase, Woodhouse, Coal-house, and Ash Tip, W.C.

Coach Houses, Harness and Saddle Rooms, four Stall Stable, and two Loose Boxes and Stable Yard.

Five Loose Boxes and Hay and Corn Store and Granary, and Lower Stable Yard.

Garage Yard

GARAGE, 42' 6" x 19' 6", WITH THREE ROOMS OVER.

Petrol Store, Barn 33' 6" x 16', Engine House, and Accumulator House.

Farm Yard

Four Pigs' Cots, three Loose Boxes, Carpenters' Shop, five-stall Stable, Cart Shed, or Garage, Blacksmiths' Shop, Harness Room, four-stall Stable and Fodder House.

Paint Shop and Slaughter-house, range of Cow Sheds to tie 14, Implement Shed, Poultry House, Saw Mill and Timber Shed, Coal Stores, Kennels.

The Gardens and Grounds

comprise : Orchard, with Apple and other fruit trees, Lawns and Ornamental Grounds ; walled Kitchen Garden with Peach House and Green-house, heated by hot water Boiler, brick Cold Frames, Potting Sheds, Bothy, Mushroom House, Stoke Hole and Stores.

Enclosed within the Kitchen Garden :

THE FIVE-ROOMED GARDENER'S COTTAGE

(stone, rough cast and tile).

Water is supplied to the Kitchen Garden by gravitation from Pwll-cae-Mynydd Pond.

Part of the Mansion House, and certain Outbuildings are in the occupation of the Glamorgan County Council (see Schedule), the remainder are in hand, or are in the occupation of Mr. O. T. Harry.

SCHEDULE.

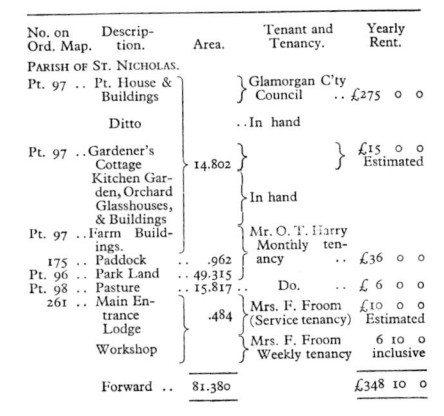

No. on Ord. Map.	Description.	Area.	Tenant and Tenancy.	Yearly Rent.
PARISH OF ST. NICHOLAS.				
Pt. 97	Pt. House & Buildings	}	Glamorgan C'ty Council	£275 0 0
	Ditto		In hand	
Pt. 97	Gardener's Cottage Kitchen Garden, Orchard Glasshouses, & Buildings	14.802	}	£15 0 0 Estimated
			In hand	
Pt. 97	Farm Buildings		Mr. O. T. Harry Monthly tenancy	
175	Paddock	.962		£36 0 0
Pt. 96	Park Land	49.315	Do.	£ 6 0 0
Pt. 98	Pasture	15.817		
261	Main Entrance Lodge	.484	Mrs. F. Froom (Service tenancy)	£10 0 0 Estimated
	Workshop		Mrs. F. Froom Weekly tenancy	6 10 0 inclusive
	Forward	81.380		£348 10 0

BELOW:
Summary of lots, 1942. (The numbers refer to the map on page 79).

To attract German bombs, decoys had been put in place: there was a **Q site,** a dummy airfield, just to the west of Cottrell and a **Starfish** installation (intended to simulate burning buildings) was just off the main road, near Wenvoe.

On 2 January 1941 over one hundred bombers were overhead. Bombs were dropped on and around Cardiff, Penarth and Barry. Llandaff Cathedral and Llandough hospital were damaged and over one hundred people were killed. Three months later Harriet Diana

Summary of Lots

LOT NO. PLAN	DESCRIPTION	AREAS
1	Cottrell House, Grounds, Cottages and Woods in hand with Gwrerddyn Farm	194.656
2	Freehold Farm, Tre-Hill, and Brook Farm and Brook Wood and Coed-y-Cwm	199.117
3	Freehold Cottage, Garden and Land, Tre-Hill Cottage	2.906
4	Freehold Cottage and Garden, Tre-Hill	.493
5	Freehold Farm, Beeches Farm	36.785
6	Freehold Accommodation Land, Tre-Hill	7.847
7	Freehold Accommodation Land, Brook Road	7.544
8	Freehold Cottage, Tre-Hill	.090
9	Do. do.	.110
10	Freehold Farm, Sheepcourt Farm and Woodland, "Coed-yr-Aber"	172.224
11	Freehold Farm, Redland and Redland Wood	119.651
12	Freehold Small Holding, Sycamore Cottage and Land	7.303
13	Freehold Cottage, Sycamore Cross	.130
14	Do. do.	.185
15	Freehold Farm, Court Farm	17.348
16	Freehold Pasture Field, Sycamore Cross	8.397
17	Do. do. do.	2.325
18	Freehold Cottage, Breach Cottage No. 1	.300
19	Freehold Cottage, Breach Cottage, No. 2	.250
20	Freehold Accommodation Land, Cottrell	34.812
21	Freehold Accommodation Land, Sycamore Cross, and Woodland	19.995
22	Freehold Accommodation Land, Sycamore Cross, Peterston-Super-Ely Road	14.952
23	Do. do. do. do.	15.873
24	Freehold Farm, Village Farm	173.838
25	Freehold Farm, Tygroes Farm	33.701
26	Freehold Accommodation Land, Bonvilston	11.660
27	Freehold Accommodation Land and Buildings, Pantyffynon	37.317
28	Freehold Farm, Pencareg and Woodland, "Coed Quinnet"	232.561
29	Freehold Farm, Blackland Farm, and Betty Lucas Wood	119.167
30	Freehold Cottage, Sheepcourt Cottages	.209
31	Do. do.	.186
32	Do. do.	.195
33	Do. Double do.	.164
34	Freehold Double Licensed Inn, Red Lion, Bonvilston	1.077
35	Freehold Blacksmith's Shop, Bonvilston	—
36	Freehold Cottage, No. 2, Red Lion Cottages, Bonvilston	.154
37	Freehold Cottage, No. 3, Do.	.176
38	Freehold Cottage, No. 4, Do.	.155
39	Freehold Garden, Bonvilston	.569
40	Freehold Cottage, Church Cottage, Bonvilston	.263
41	Bonvilston Post Office and Garden	.473
42	Freehold Pasture Field and Garden, Bonvilston	7.460
43	Freehold Accommodation Land, Logwood Hill, Peterston-Super-Ely, Trehedyn Land	37.660
44	Freehold Accommodation Pasture Land, Sycamore Cross—Pendoylan Road	18.211
45	Freehold Accommodation Pasture Land, Trehedyn Land, Peterston-Super-Ely	4.120
46	Do. do. do. do.	14.047
47	Do. do. do. do.	2.589
48	Do. do. do. do.	2.399
49	Do. do. Pendoylan Moors	1.657
50	Leasehold Dwelling House, Gwern-y-Steeple	
51	Do. do. do.	
	TOTAL ACRES	1,563.301

LEFT:
The sale particulars, 1942.

COTTRELL

BELOW:
The estate, as let, in 1942.

Arabella Mary Mackintosh died, in the house where she had been born eighty-four years earlier. The first clause of her will was "I desire that my body may be buried in the family vault at Petty Church, near Inverness". In 1942, the Cottrell estate was sold.

Schedule of Estate as Let

TENANT	HOLDING	AREA	RENT £ s. d.	REMARKS
FREEHOLDS.				
Glamorgan County Council.	Cottrell Mansion and Grounds, Buildings, Stables, Garage, etc.	14.802	275 0 0	
In Hand	Part House and Buildings.			
In Hand	Gardener's Cottage,		15 0 0	Service Tenancy Estim'td
	Kitchen Garden, Orchard, Glasshouses, and Buildings			
In Hand	Main Entrance Lodge.	.484	10 0 0	Service Tenancy Estim'td
F. Froom	Work Shop		6 10 0	Inclusive
In Hand	Woodlands around Cottrell.	41.558	—	
O. T. Harry	Cottrell Farm Buildings, Paddock and Parklands.	50.277	36 0 0	
O. T. Harry	Pasture Land	15.817	6 0 0	
E. J. Dunn	Gwreiddyn Farm.	61.066	55 0 0	
E. J. Dunn	Pasture	10.652	10 10 0	
W. T. Bassett	Tre-Hill Farm	215.873	220 0 0	
In Hand	Woodland	12.286	—	
W. T. Bassett	Tre-Hill Cottage.	.455	10 10 10	
W. Payne	Cottage, Tre-Hill.	.493	20 0 0	
O. T. Harry	Beeches Farm	24.585	38 5 10	
In Hand	Old Quarry	1.000		
Thos. Cule	Cottage, Tre-Hill.	.090	8 0 0	
W. Coles	Cottage, Tre-Hill.	.110	7 16 0	Inclusive
James James	Sheepcourt Farm and Redland Farm	286.210	243 9 0	
In Hand	Woodland	16.387	—	
R. J. Knowles	Small Holding, Sycamore Cottage and Land.	7.303	25 6 6	
A. Ranger	Cottage, Sycamore Cross.	.130	13 0 0	
Mrs. G. M. Littley.	Sheepcourt Hill Cottage.	.185	10 3 0	
T. B. Evans	Court Farm	85.379	120 6 0	
In Hand	Woodland	1.000		
	Carried forward	846.142	1,130 17 2	

TENANT	HOLDING	AREA	RENT £ s. d.	REMARKS
FREEHOLDS—continued.	*Brought forward*	846.142	1,130 17 2	
P. Tanner	Breach Cottage No. 1	.300	19 10 0	
Mrs. J. Flynn	Breach	.250	19 10 0	
James James	Pasture Land	34.032	30 12 0	
In Hand	Woodland	.780	—	
A. T. Evans	Village Farm	173.838	179 4 3	
W. T. Miles	Ty-Groes and Pantyffynon Farm.	81.725	121 10 0	
In Hand	Roadway and Rough.	.953		
D. R. Griffiths	Pen-careg Farm.	192.422	100 0 0	
In Hand	Woodland	40.139	—	
J. Thomas	Blackland Farm.	113.058	97 13 0	
In Hand	Woodland	6.109	—	
G. Prickett	Sheepcourt Cottage.	.209	13 0 0	
Mrs. E. Evans	Sheepcourt Cottage.	.186	13 0 0	
D. John	Sheepcourt Cottage.	.195	13 0 0	
R. Gartshore	Sheepcourt Cottage	.164	13 0 0	
E. C. Decre	Red Lion Inn and Paddock.	1.077	49 19 0	
Ed. Davies	Blacksmith's Shop.	—	12 0 0	
L. G. Williams, Trustees.	No. 2, Red Lion Cottages	.154	10 14 0	Under Lease. Apportioned.
L. G. Williams, Trustees.	No. 3, Red Lion Cottages	.176	10 14 0	
L. G. Williams, Trustees.	No. 4, Red Lion Cottages	.155	10 14 0	
R. H. Williams	Garden	.569	5 0 0	Under Lease.
A. H. Jenkins	Church Cottage.	.263	52 0 0	
C. Farmer	Bonvilston Post Office.	.473	22 0 0	
L. G. Williams, Trustees.	Pasture Field and Garden	7.460	16 10 0	
H. David	Trehedyn Land.	50.160	67 4 6	
I. Thomas	Garden	1.251	1 0 0	
In Hand	Woodlands	11.061	—	
LEASEHOLDS.				
E. H. Rees	Dwellinghouse, Gwern-y-Steeple.	—	18 4 0	
H. C. Coles	Dwellinghouse, Gwern-y-Steeple.	—	18 4 0	
	TOTAL	1563.301	2,044 19 11	

With two exceptions as shown, the tenants pay rates in all cases.

8. William Powell and Sons

ABOVE:
The SS Hillglade, in 1926, bringing 49,000 bags of sugar for William Powell & Sons - the first direct cargo of Canadian sugar to south Wales.

The Cottrell estate was bought by William Powell and Sons in September 1942, but the mansion and other buildings were under war-time occupation, being used by Glamorgan County Council as an emergency fire-station and stores.

William Powell and Sons began trading in 1874 and built up an extensive business as importers of provisions and canned goods, being among the first to bring in Libby's products from the United States. They took over the Cardiff firms of Collett Whitfield and John Isaac, and owned a number of local properties including farms at Greendown and Culverhouse in addition to their provision warehouse at Colonial House (62-66 Millicent Street) and their general warehouse in Tredegar Street, Cardiff. A limited company was set up in 1926 and another building was acquired, in 1928, when a London base was opened at 194 Borough High Street, Southwark (near to Libby's London office). The building was given up in the early 1930s.

The directors of the company at the time of the purchase of Cottrell were William Johns-Powell (son of the founder) and his

William Powell and Sons en fête. The van is decorated with British and American flags and the words "Well done". This may be a celebration of the first solo flight across the Atlantic, by Charles Lindbergh, in May 1927.

BELOW: *The Cumberland* discharging butter for William Powell and Sons. This was (1927) the first direct shipment of Australian butter for south Wales.

WILLIAM POWELL AND SONS

194 Borough High Street, Southwark. A photograph of William Powell's London branch taken in 1929.

LEFT: *Front row (left to right): Anne Peace Arabella Mackintosh (grand-daughter of The Mackintosh), Serena Boothby, Ann Homfray. With the top hat: Neville Johns-Powell.*

FAR LEFT: *"D' ye ken Johns-Powell?" William Johns-Powell with John Peel's hunting horn, bought at Sotheby's in 1951.*

brothers Oscar and Dapho. In December 1951 William became the object of considerable local, national and international press attention - he bought John Peel's hunting horn at Sotheby's (purchase price: £600). In the following year the horn was flown to the United States, where it was a big attraction at the 23rd Annual Chicagoland Music Festival sponsored by *Chicago Tribune* Charities Inc. On the Saturday (23rd August 1952) the horn was blown, before 70,000 people at Soldiers' Field, by Patric Aidan Regan of Barrington, Illinois: "champion hunt caller of the middle western hunt clubs" and whipper-in of the Fox River Valley Hunt.

Oscar died in 1948 and William's son, Neville, was made a

121

Clanyon on the way to winning the 1959 Topham Trophy. The other horse is ESB.

director in the following year. Neville Johns-Powell was an enthusiastic horseman, adopting as his racing colours "dark red, with gold horse shoes and a black cap". In 1935, at the age of eighteen, he took part in the Glamorgan Hunt Point-to-Point races at Crossways (near Cowbridge), winning the Members' Race on his *Zealous Jenny*. This success was repeated in the following year, by which time he was - while an undergraduate at Cambridge - Master and Huntsman of the Cambridgeshire Harriers (founded in 1745). He continued to ride in point-to-points until the outbreak of war, when he joined the army, serving in the middle east.

Although riding in some local races after the war, Neville Johns-Powell turned increasingly towards a training role. In 1953 *Clanyon* - bought as a yearling at Newmarket - won the Adjacent Hunts' race of the Pentyrch Hunt meeting at St. Fagans. Later to be described as "tough, consistent and rarely runs badly", *Clanyon* went on to win more prominent races, including the Topham Trophy in March 1959. (The distance was 2 miles and 6 furlongs over part of the Grand National course.) A year later *Clanyon* ran in the Grand National itself as "one of the longest-priced horses" but did not finish that very

WILLIAM POWELL AND SONS

BELOW:
Cottrell on 21 July 1967. The mansion, stables and outbuildings are prominent. The walled-garden stands out clearly, with the gardener's house at its bottom right-hand corner (near what is now the first tee of the Button course). The driving range was built in the paddock at the bottom of the picture, with the golf clubhouse and car park to the right.

demanding course.

Neville's wife, Patricia Johns-Powell, formed the Cottrell Park Stud in 1969, in order to breed Welsh Ponies. They have been exported to many parts of the world including Australia, New Zealand, North America, Holland, Germany and Sweden. Mrs. Johns-Powell served as President of the Welsh Pony and Cob Society in 1998.

Neville Johns-Powell died in 1976 and the provisions-importing business was sold in the following year. The Cottrell estate was retained and devoted to mixed farming until 1994, when development of the golf courses began. About sixty per cent of the estate is now given over to golf, including two courses - the Button and the Mackintosh - and a floodlit driving range. Construction work took

COTTRELL

Construction of the golf courses began in 1994.

1996. The first of June, the first tee, the first drive (by Mike Pycroft).

nearly two years, and the courses were formally declared open by Sara Edwards (of BBC Wales Television) on 1st June 1996. The first drive, from the first tee of the Button course, was made by the Club Professional, Mike Pycroft.

Today, thanks to a thriving Golf Club, more people than ever are able to enjoy the beautiful parkland of Cottrell, which is still owned and managed by one family, as it has been for over five hundred years: Merrick, Button, Gwinnett, Tyler, Mackintosh, and Johns-Powell.

COTTRELL

APPENDIX

OWNERS OF COTTRELL

Meurig ap Howell	1546 - 1558
Rice Merrick	1558 - 1587
Morgan Merrick	1587 - 1624
Barbara Merrick	1624 - c.1640
Miles Button	c.1640 - ?
Thomas Button	? - 1710
Thomas Button	1710 - 1718
Barbara Button	1718 - 1755
Emilia Button	1755
Samuel Gwinnett	1755 - 1792
Emilia Gwinnett	1792 - 1807
Earl of Clarendon	1807 - 1824
Sir George Tyler	1824 - 1862
(Sir Charles Tyler, tenant)	1817 - 1835)
Lady Tyler	1862 - 1873
George Henry Tyler	1873 - 1878
Gwinnett Tyler	1878 - 1886
George William Tyler	1886
Harriet D.A.M. Mackintosh	1886 - 1941
William Powell and Sons	1942 - present

SOURCES

This book is intended for the general reader, so I have not provided the usual scholarly apparatus of footnotes to the text. Listed below are the main written sources of information which have helped to build up this outline history of the families connected with Cottrell.

MERRICK

Cottrell Papers in the Glamorgan Record Office.

Rice Merrick **Morganiae Archaeographia: A Book of Glamorganshire's Antiquities.** (Ed. Brian Ll. James, 1983).

Gwynnedd O. Pierce (1968) **The Place Names of Dinas Powys Hundred.** (University of Wales Press.).

Margaret Robbins (1974) **The Agricultural, Domestic, Social and Cultural Interests of the Gentry in South-East Glamorgan 1540-1640.** (PhD thesis, University of Wales).

Royal Commission on Ancient and Historical Monuments in Wales (1991) **An Inventory of the Ancient Monuments in Glamorgan.** Vol. III. Part 1a. (HMSO).

Glanmor Williams (Ed) **Glamorgan County History.** Vol. IV: Early Modern Glamorgan.

SIR THOMAS BUTTON

Some of Sir Thomas Button's correspondence is in the Public Record Office, and in **Calendar of State Papers (Domestic)** and **Calendar of State Papers (Ireland).**

K.R. Andrews (1954) 'Christopher Newport of Limehouse, Mariner' **William and Mary Quarterly**, xi, pp.28-41.

Kenneth R. Andrews (Ed) (1959) **English Privateering Voyages to the West Indies 1588-1595.** (Hakluyt Society / Cambridge U.P.).

G.N. Clark (1944) 'The Barbary Corsairs in the Seventeenth Century' **Cambridge Historical Journal,** VIII, No.1, pp.22-35.

G.T. Clark (1862) 'Some account of the parishes of St. Nicholas and St. Lythans' **Archaeologia Cambrensis.** Third Series. July 1862. pp.177-196.

G.T. Clark (1883) **Some Account of Sir Robert Mansel and of Admiral Sir Thomas Button.** (Dowlais).

Dictionary of National Biography.

Margaret Robbins (1974) **The Agricultural, Domestic, Social and Cultural Interests of the Gentry in South-East Glamorgan 1540-1640.** (PhD thesis, University of Wales).

N.A.M. Rodger (1997) **The Safeguard of the Sea: A Naval History of Britain. Volume I: 660-1649.** (Harper Collins / National Maritime Museum).

Charles F. Shepherd (1967) 'Admiral Sir Thomas Button' in **Stewart Williams's Glamorgan Historian** Vol.4, pp.121-135.

Glanmor Williams (1998) **Renewal and Reformation: Wales c.1415-1642.** (Oxford U.P.).

Daniel Woodward (Ed) (1973) 'Sir Thomas Button, the *Phoenix* and the defence of the Irish coast 1614-1622' **The Mariner's Mirror,** Vol.59, No.2, pp.343-344.

BUTTON

Cottrell papers in the Glamorgan Record Office.

Barbara Button's will is in the National Library of Wales.

Thanks to Arwyn Lloyd Hughes for the quotation from William Price of Rhiwlas.

Charles Carlton (1992) **Going to the Wars: The Experience of the British Civil Wars 1638-1651.** (Routledge).

Peter Gaunt (1991) **A Nation Under Siege: The Civil War in Wales 1642-48.** (Cadw).

S.R. Gardiner (1898) **History of the Great Civil War 1642-1649.** (4 vols.) (Longmans).

Philip Jenkins (1983) **The Making of a Ruling Class: The Glamorgan Gentry 1640-1790.** (Cambridge U.P.).

Felicity Neal and Clive Holmes (1994) **The Gentry in England and Wales.** (Macmillan).

P.R. Newman (1981) **Royalist Officers in England and Wales 1642-1660: A Biographical Dictionary.** (New York/London: Garland).

J.R. Phillips (1874) **Memoirs of the Civil War in Wales and the Marches 1642-1649.** (2 vols.). (Longmans).

S.A. Raymond (1980) 'The Glamorgan Arraymen' **Morgannwg** XXIV, pp.9-30.

B.W. Richards (1989) 'Colonel Poyer and relatives: Some mistaken assumptions' **Dyfed Family History Society Journal** April 1989. pp.67-72.

C.F. Shepherd (1934) **St. Nicholas: A Historical Survey of a Glamorganshire Parish.** (Cardiff).

C. Mervyn Thomas 'The Civil Wars in Glamorgan' in Glanmor Williams (Ed) (1974) **Glamorgan County History.** Vol. IV Early Modern Glamorgan.

Hilary M. Thomas (1989) 'Llandough Castle, near Cowbridge' **Morgannwg** XXXIII, pp.7-36.

GWINNETT

Samuel Gwinnett

Gloucester Library has some manuscripts of Sam Gwinnett (the younger). His marriage contract is in the National Library of Wales.

R.T.W. Denning (Ed) (1995) **The Diary of William Thomas 1762-1795.** (South Wales Record Society).

Philip Jenkins (1983) **The Making of a Ruling Class: The Glamorgan Gentry 1640-1790.** (Cambridge U.P.).

Button Gwinnett

Kenneth Coleman (1958) **The American Revolution in Georgia 1763-1789.** (University of Georgia).

Kenneth Coleman (ed) (1977) **A History of Georgia.**

Harold E. Davis (1976) **The Fledgling Province: Social and Cultural Life in Georgia 1733-1776.**

C.F. Jenkins (1926) **Button Gwinnett: Signer of the Declaration of Independence.** (New York: Doubleday, Page).

The New Georgia Guide. (1996).

D.R. Paterson 'Button Gwinnett and his family associations with Glamorgan' **Transactions of Cardiff Naturalists' Society** LXVI pp.69-80.

John Price Gwinnett

His will is in the Public Record Office.

V.C.P. Hodson **List of Officers of the Bengal Army.**

Emilia Gwinnett

Public Record Office: Lady Vernon's will; Emilia Gwinnett's will; Chancery case judgement.

British Library: The Sotheby's sale catalogue.

B. Ll James (1971) **The Vale of Glamorgan** 1780-1850. (Master's degree thesis, University of Wales).

William Linnard (1987) 'John Perkins of Llantrithyd. The diary of a gentleman farmer in the Vale of Glamorgan 1788-1801' **Morgannwg** XXXI pp.9-36.

John Newman (1995) **The Buildings of Wales: Glamorgan.** (Penguin/University of Wales Press.).

Hilary M. Thomas (Ed) **The Diaries of John Bird.** (South Wales Record Society).

Hilary M. Thomas (1997) 'Llanmihangel, near Cowbridge: A tale of family fortunes and misfortunes' **Morgannwg** XLI pp.9-37.

James Phelp

A few papers in the Leicestershire Record Office.

R.J. Colyer (1980) 'Nanteos: A landed estate in decline 1800-1930' **Ceredigion** IX.

W.J. Lewis (1960) 'Some aspects of the history of Aberystwyth II' **Ceredigion** IV ,No.1.

TYLER

Charles Tyler

The National Maritime Museum has papers presented in 1952 by Mrs. I.M. Bond, a descendant. They consist of service documents, letters received, and letters to Lady Tyler 1800-1815.

Geoffrey Bennett (1977) **The Battle of Trafalgar.** (Batsford).

William Laird Clowes (1899 and 1900) **The Royal Navy: A History.** Vols. IV and V. (Samson Low).

Dictionary of National Biography.

Cyril Field (1924) **Britain's Sea Soldiers.** Vol.I. (Liverpool: Lyceum Press).

Robert Gardiner (Ed) **Fleet Battle and Blockade: The French Revolutionary War 1793-97.** (Chatham).

Robert Gardiner (1996) **Navies and the American Revolution 1775-1783.** (Chatham).

John D. Harbron (1988) **Trafalgar and the Spanish Navy.** (Conway).

Brian Lavery (1989) **Nelson's Navy: The Ships, Men and Organisation 1793-1815.** (Conway).

C. Rathbone Low (1884) **Her Majesty's Navy, including Its Deeds and Battles.** Vol.III (London).

R.H. Mackenzie (1913) **The Trafalgar Roll.** (London).

J. Marshall (1823) **Naval Biography.** Vol.1. Part I.

Peter Philip (1981) **British Residents at the Cape 1795-1819.** (Cape Town).

R.E.R. Robinson (1988) **The Bloody Eleventh: History of the Devonshire Regiment.** Vol.I 1685-1815. (Exeter).

N.A.M. Rodger (1986) **The Wooden World: An Anatomy of the Georgian Navy.** (Collins).

Alan Schom (1992) **Trafalgar: Countdown to Battle 1803-1805.** (Penguin).

G.M. Theal (1964) **History of South Africa 1795-1872.** Vol. 5. (Cape Town).

Roland Thorne (1981) 'The Leach family of Castlemartin' **The Pembrokeshire Historian** No.7. pp.29-51.

W.H. Wyndham-Quin (1912) **Sir Charles Tyler, GCB, Admiral of the White.** (London).

George Tyler

I would like to express special thanks to Neil Walklate (Cowbridge) who generously made available the results of his researches into the history of the parish of St. Nicholas. Thanks also to Thomas Lloyd and E. Thomas for information about David Vaughan.

Glamorgan Record Office - census returns.

National Library of Wales - David Vaughan's journal is at NLW 20149C; tithe surveys and maps.

Thomas Lloyd (1989) **Lost Houses of Wales.**

John Newman (1995) **Buildings of Wales: Glamorgan.**

William R. O'Byrne (1849) **A Naval Biographical Dictionary.** (London).

George Henry Tyler

His will and service record are in the Public Record Office.

Gwinnett Tyler and George William Tyler

Service records are in the Public Record Office. **The London Gazette.**

MACKINTOSH

The Scottish Record Office has some documents in the Fraser Mackintosh collection (GD 128) and in Mackintosh Muniments (GD 176). These include personal letters to Mrs. Mackintosh, several of which solicit her support for local activities. There is also an account from Chas. E. Hardyman and E. Sutton Smith for medical attendance for family and household (1889), and an estimate from Wood Bros. (Cardiff) for conveyance of furniture from Cottrell to within three miles of Paddington Station (1890).

Public Record Office: Census returns, and the army record of The Mackintosh.

Ministry of Transport: **Report of Accident Inquiry** (17 August 1936).

Articles in **Glasgow Herald, Inverness Courier, The Scotsman, Western Mail.**

John Davies (1981) **Cardiff and the Marquesses of Bute.**

Charles Deere **The Recollections of Charles Deere of Bonvilston.** (Typescript).

Horn and Hound in Wales and Some Adjoining Counties. (Cardiff: 1891).

Brian Ll James (1981) **The Development of the Mackintosh (Plasnewydd) Estate in Roath.** (Typescript in Cardiff City Library).

Brian Lee (1986) **The Races Came Off: The Story of Point-to-Point Racing in South and South-West Wales 1887-1985.**

Margaret Mackintosh of Mackintosh (Revised Edtn. 1982) **The History of the Clan Mackintosh and the Clan Chattan.** (Edinburgh).

Pauline McGillivray (1985) 'Mackintoshes in Wales' in **Clan Chattan: Journal of the Clan Chattan Association.** VIII(3). pp.166-168.

Robert McGillivray (1981) 'A memorable occasion - The coming-of-age of Angus Mackintosh' in **Clan Chattan: Journal of the Clan Chattan Association.** VII(5). pp.262-262.

C.J. Parry (1996) **The Story of the Order of St. John in Wales.** (Hospitallers Club of Wales).

William Ramsey (Ed) (1988) **The Blitz: Then and Now.**

Kenneth Rose (1983) **King George V** includes the story of the king and The Mackintosh's grand-daughter.